Part-time Faculty:
Higher Education at a Crossroads

by Judith M. Gappa

ASHE-ERIC Higher Education Research Report No. 3, 1984

Prepared by

 ® *Clearinghouse on Higher Education*
The George Washington University

Published by

Association for the Study of Higher Education

Jonathan D. Fife,
Series Editor

LB
2335.35
·637
1984

Cite as:
Gappa, Judith M. *Part-time Faculty: Higher Education at a Crossroads*. ASHE-ERIC Higher Education Research Report No. 3. Washington, D.C.: Association for the Study of Higher Education, 1984.

The ERIC Clearinghouse on Higher Education invites individuals to submit proposals for writing monographs for the Higher Education Research Report series. Proposals must include:
1. A detailed manuscript proposal of not more than five pages.
2. A 75-word summary to be used by several review committees for the initial screening and rating of each proposal.
3. A vita.
4. A writing sample.

Library of Congress Catalog Card Number: 84-72775
ISSN 0737-1292
ISBN 0-913317-12-8

ᴱᴿᴵᶜ° Clearinghouse on Higher Education
The George Washington University
One Dupont Circle, Suite 630
Washington, D.C. 20036

ᴬˢᴴᴱ Association for the Study of Higher Education
One Dupont Circle, Suite 630
Washington, D.C. 20036

This publication was partially prepared with funding from the National Institute of Education, U.S. Department of Education, under contract no. 400-82-0011. The opinions expressed in this report do not necessarily reflect the positions or policies of NIE or the Department.

EXECUTIVE SUMMARY

More than a quarter million part-time faculty are employed in American colleges and universities (NCES 1980). A reasonable guess is that they carry 15 percent of the total college-level teaching load. Most part-timers are poorly paid, have marginal job security at best, and get little institutional support for their teaching efforts. Nearly all to some extent resent the uncollegial treatment they receive and are frustrated by the impediments to good teaching performance they must put up with. But on balance, they are sufficiently satisfied to continue. Some teach more for the prestige it provides in relation to their full-time careers than for the money. Few rely wholly on part-time teaching for their livelihoods.

Policy issues regarding part-time faculty are clouded and complicated by problems with definitions and data. Federal data are inadequate and not regularly updated; state studies are seldom compatible, either with federal studies or with one another. Independent studies are infrequent and usually too limited in scope to support generalizations. And no major study has been undertaken since the late 1970s. Available statistics about academic qualifications, personal characteristics, professional aspirations, teaching loads, and compensation are sparse and out of date.

How Do Part-time Faculty Affect the Quality of Academic Programs?

The number of part-time faculty has steadily increased over the past three decades, and their role in higher education may well expand further in coming years. By 1980, 32 percent of all faculty were part-timers (NCES 1980). Fifty-three percent of these part-timers are in two-year colleges, 34 percent are in four-year colleges, and 13 percent are in universities (Eliason 1980; Tuckman 1978). Therefore, their teaching performance can and does affect the overall quality of academic programs. Institutions by and large have not recognized that part-time faculty can be a major asset to their academic programs. Part-timers are painfully aware that administrators and full-time faculty see them as second-class citizens. The increased numbers of part-timers pose a challenge:

The jury remains out on the question of whether part-timers augment the quality of higher education or whether they debase it. Whether they will become a larger force in the next two decades will depend, in large part, on the policies that institutions of higher education will adopt in the next few years. Part-timers are neither good nor bad for academe in their own right. Instead they are a diverse group with many different motives and goals. Whether we learn to employ them in a constructive manner will surely be one of the most fascinating questions of the '80's (Tuckman and Tuckman 1981, p. 7).

What Influences Institutional Policies and Practices for the Employment of Part-time Faculty?

Policies and practices are shaped by the diverse characteristics of part-timers; by institutional needs, missions, and traditions; by the academic labor market; and by legal and collective bargaining constraints.

Part-time faculty vary widely in their reasons for seeking part-time employment, their faculty roles, and their career aspirations. A large study in 1976–77 by Howard Tuckman and associates identified seven categories of part-timers, ranging from semiretired academics to people whose principal occupation is homemaking. Many part-timers are employed full time in other occupations and teach part time for personal satisfaction. Others put together two or more part-time teaching jobs that add up to full-time work. Graduate students and those who hold advanced degrees but cannot find full-time teaching positions are the most dissatisfied part-timers, in part because they are most strongly motivated to pursue full-time academic careers (Tuckman 1978). Part-timers can be categorized according to their primary motivation for teaching part-time; in order of importance, these motives are personal satisfaction, enhancement of one's nonacademic profession, aspirations for a full-time traditional academic career, and economic (Leslie, Kellams, and Gunne 1982).

The reasons for employing part-timers also vary based upon institutions' needs and missions. The largest number of part-time faculty are employed by community colleges, where they slightly outnumber full-time faculty. Community colleges must meet local demand for courses and programs of immediate interest—credit and noncredit, on and off campus. Part-time faculty are an integral part of the community college's effectiveness, and they generally have been accorded more respect and better treatment than those teaching in four-year institutions. Scattered efforts by institutions to give part-timers more teaching support and improve their morale have nearly all been in two-year colleges.

In four-year institutions, the ratio of part-time to full-time faculty is roughly one to three (Tuckman 1978). The flexibility and savings in costs that part-timers provide have been most important to small private schools. Part-timers have also been employed extensively in urban universities with large enrollments of part-time adult students. These universities are able to staff many programs with the rare concentration of talent available in urban areas. In universities with graduate programs and a supply of graduate teaching assistants, employment of part-time faculty has been less prevalent (Leslie, Kellams, and Gunne 1982; Tuckman and Vogler 1978).

What Are the Constraints on the Employment of Part-time Faculty?

Two Supreme Court cases set legal precedent regarding the rights of part-time faculty: *Perry* v. *Sinderman* [408 U.S. 593 (1972)] and *Board of Regents* v. *Roth* [408 U.S. 564 (1972)]. The controlling precedents for these cases established that part-timers may be able to claim property rights not explicitly granted by an institution but accruing from policy, common practice, or acquiescence, and that part-timers do not have a right to due process in the non-renewal or termination of employment unless they can show that they have property rights. And most part-time faculty contracts make it very difficult for part-timers to establish property rights (Head 1979; Leslie, Kellams, and Gunne 1982).

Suits alleging denial of equal protection under the law have been largely unsuccessful. Institutions can argue that part-timers perform fewer tasks than full-time faculty and are employed on genuinely different terms; thus, a rational basis exists for unequal pay and benefits.

Collective bargaining affects the status of part-time faculty through decisions whether or not to include part-time faculty in bargaining units (Leslie and Ikenberry 1979). About 41 percent of all public-sector collective bargaining units include at least some part-timers, whereas only 28 percent of private-sector units do (Leslie, Kellams, and Gunne 1982). While the primary beneficiaries of collective bargaining have been full-time faculty, at least some part-timers have achieved more equitable compensation and improved working conditions as a result of contract negotiations.

What Conclusions and Recommendations Emerge from the Study of Part-time Faculty?

The idea that the employment of part-time faculty is a casual departmental affair rather than a planned institutional effort is obsolete. If educational quality is to be promoted and preserved, an institution's legitimate academic and financial needs must be balanced by the equally legitimate demands of part-time faculty for improved status, compensation, and services (Head 1979).

Expanded research and dissemination of information about part-time faculty at the institutional, state, regional, and national levels can lead to recognition of their importance and to revision of institutional policies and practices for their employment. Institutional researchers and higher education scholars need to examine part-time faculty employment as an integral part of their studies of faculty working conditions and careers (Brown 1982; Emmet 1981; Stern et al. 1981).

Institutional policies and practices should take into account the differences among part-time faculty in their qualifications, the functions they perform, and their contributions to the school's educational objectives. Institutions should replace freewheeling departmental autonomy with centralized responsibility and accountability for part-time faculty employment to ensure fair and humane treatment (Leslie, Kellams, and Gunne 1982). With centralized responsibility, institutions can establish policies and procedures that differentiate among part-timers, based on their individual characteristics and the reasons for which they were employed. These policies and practices should encompass recruitment and hiring, assignment and workload, support services, participation in governance, compensation, fringe benefits, and job security.

The challenge is not to provide parity with full-time faculty. Instead, it is to establish clearly articulated, well-understood, humane, and equitable policies and practices that accommodate the variety among part-timers themselves (Head 1979; Smith 1980; Stern et al. 1981; Wallace 1982). Institutional policies and practices should place less emphasis upon a polarization between full-time, tenured faculty and part-time, temporary faculty. Faculty employment policies and practices should constitute a continuum embracing the total group: from full-time, tenured faculty to fully qualified, continuing part-time faculty interested in their teaching careers to contingency faculty hired to meet the demands of enrollment.

CONTENTS

FOREWORD

The issue of part-time faculty is controversial, partly because all arguments are compelling and partly because
both faculty and administrators acknowledge that there are
both benefits and threats to the institution and educational
mission.

Two prominent arguments support the use of part-time
faculty. The first is that it increases staffing flexibility. Part-
timers allow an institution to meet unexpected student
overloads in curriculum areas that are in vogue, or to provide necessary expertise in rapidly developing areas in
which full-time faculty have not been able to keep up.
They may enhance an institution's reputation: "stars" can
teach occasionally while they are employed full-time in
other sectors such as business and government. Part-time
faculty may bring specific skills, experiences, or insight—
gained through their primary occupations—that full-timers
do not have.

The second reason for the employment of part-time faculty is economic. Since they are normally paid less than
full-time faculty, institutions can provide quality education
at a lower cost. This translated into lower tuitions and
higher enrollments. The long-term effect is improved institutional solvency and greater job security for full-time
faculty.

Criticisms against the use of part-time faculty also fall
into two categories. The first argument is that because of
time demands of their other employment, part-time personnel are unable to give the necessary attention to their academic responsibilities. It is contended that part-time faculty are often poorly prepared and not available to properly
counsel and advise students, lack loyalty to the institution,
and do not contribute to the other two missions of the
institution—teaching and research. The second argument is
that part-time faculty are more easily manipulated by the
administration and therefore threaten the influence of full-
time faculty in the decision making and policy making
process.

The circumstances facing institutions during the next
decade, especially budgetary and curricular problems, will
necessitate the use of part-time faculty. The question
therefore is not whether institutions should utilize part-
time faculty, but how best can institutions use them. This
report by Judith M. Gappa, Associate Provost for Faculty

Affairs at San Francisco State University, contributes to a greater understanding of the current use of part-time faculty and the issues that surround them. Through definitive analysis analysis of the available research and literature, she offers insight into the current dimension of the use of part-time faculty, their motivations to serve, and institutional policy, practices, and related constraints.

This controversy is not a passing one. As the haphazard use of part-time faculty grows, so will the conflict intensify. Gappa's report provides a firm foundation for administrative and faculty committees to establish long-term policies and practices that will maximize the use of part-time faculty while minimizing their negative effect on institutional goals and missions.

Jonathan D. Fife
Series Editor
Professor and Director
ERIC Clearinghouse on Higher Education
The George Washington University

ACKNOWLEDGMENTS

The author wishes to express her appreciation to Richard Chait for his rigorous review of the first draft and numerous thoughtful suggestions, to William Johnston for his sensitivity and dedication to the topic while editing the manuscript, and to Richard Hasbany for his cheerful optimism and limitless patience throughout countless revisions. The author is also indebted to Jonathan Fife and the staff of the ERIC Clearinghouse on Higher Education for their assistance in searching the literature.

INTRODUCTION

Part-time Teaching: Scope and Status

Higher education is one of the largest enterprises in America. In the mid-1980s, colleges and universities will be spending well over $60 billion a year on operations, and about 80 percent of the typical institutional operating budget goes to remunerate faculty and other personnel. The National Center for Education Statistics (NCES) estimates that nationwide nearly one in every three faculty is employed part time—or more than a quarter million people. (An exact count is not possible because a standard definition of "part-time faculty" does not exist.) Part-timers do not do one-third of the teaching, of course. But they do a substantial amount of it—a fair guess is 15 percent—and some work full time by teaching at two or three different schools.

The role of part-timers in determining the quality and relevance of instructional programs is therefore a matter of importance to all concerned with the operation and effectiveness of this huge enterprise, from policy makers to students. But for many reasons, including some that institutional administrators and tenured faculty would rather not discuss, part-time faculty have not been the subject of comprehensive study and evaluation. Colleges and universities have been content, by and large, to pay them poorly, use them as needed with little concern for their long-term welfare, and keep them outside traditional academic governance. Many within the tenured cloister regard part-time faculty as academic pariahs. Administrators exploit them with impunity—and apparently with almost no sense of guilt.

Nationwide nearly one in every three faculty is employed part time.

But their numbers do not diminish, and their role in higher education may well enlarge in coming years. In varying degrees, part-timers are resentful and frustrated (with much justification), but on balance, they are satisfied enough to continue. Less interested in money than in the other rewards they associate with teaching, they rarely complain.

The following chapters provide a compendium of what is known about part-time faculty, their demographic and employment characteristics, the policies and practices that institutions follow for part-time employment, and legal and other constraints influencing the way they are used. They catalog some institutional efforts to improve the status and use of part-time faculty and explore some implications for policy.

The reader must be warned that extrapolation and surmise play a large role in the author's efforts to create a coherent picture of part-time faculty. No aspect of higher education has been more neglected than part-time teaching, and as a result virtually all the available statistics are out of date. Data from the studies that are available are not fully compatible or comparable. Community colleges are disproportionately represented in the literature, because that sector of higher education is where the most effort has been expended to obtain information about part-timers and to facilitate their effectiveness. Nevertheless, this monograph seeks to make the most of what information is at hand, without pretending to have exhausted the subject.

Then and Now

Until well into the nineteenth century, the typical American college teacher was a minister, schooled in the classical portion of the liberal arts curriculum. He was most likely a young clergyman, teaching part time while awaiting a full-time ministerial appointment. Full-time lay faculty were rare.

As the twentieth century approached, the development of universities and the expansion of undergraduate and advanced curricula in a growing number of special fields created a demand for new and different kinds of faculty. Full-time college teaching emerged as an accepted profession for laymen with adequate credentials. The once-dominant figure of the young minister teaching the classics all but faded from view in higher education.

But part-time teaching did not thereby lose stature. The multiplying, ever-narrowing areas of specialization in most fields created widespread need for part-time teachers with expertise in a specific area. At most institutions, full-time faculty positions could not be justified for many areas of specialization that nonetheless needed to be taught. Experts were engaged to teach part time, and institutions exchanged visiting scholars to broaden their offerings. In the professional fields, such as medicine, law, or education, distinguished practitioners were appointed as adjunct faculty. They sometimes taught, but more often they supervised internships and practica (Blackburn 1978, pp. 100–101). Their numbers were limited, and they were concentrated in graduate and professional programs.

The full-time, campus-based faculty member has been the predominant figure in American higher education throughout this century. But since World War II, the use of part-time faculty has been vastly extended, for various reasons. The underlying cause was the unprecedented growth in all sectors of higher education that began in the late 1950s. Despite pell-mell expansion of graduate programs, the production of adequately credentialed scholars and researchers bent on academic careers did not catch up with demand in most fields until the mid-1970s. In applied mathematics and a few other specialties associated with high technology, shortages have continued into the 1980s. Where full-timers were not available, part-timers were hired. Liberal arts colleges and other schools that could not attract all the full-time faculty they needed often employed faculty members' spouses to teach part time. The faculty wife with a graduate degree could in that way accommodate the prevailing notion that her first obligation was to her family and home while still pursuing professional work (Blackburn 1978; Yang and Zak 1981). The ability to offer part-time teaching to a spouse became a recruiting device for schools with otherwise limited resources for compensation.

The burgeoning community college sector was particularly motivated to hire part-timers. Part-timers provided the great flexibility needed to offer the large assortment of vocational and technical programs available at low cost— with or without academic credit, day or night, on or off campus (Blackburn 1978; Yang and Zak 1981). Unrostered part-time instructors, used as needed and often fully employed in business or industry, facilitated expansion at a time when community colleges were least able to compete for teachers bent on academic careers. Today, roughly half of all faculty in community colleges teach only part time.

In the 1970s, the smaller four-year institutions and later virtually all colleges and universities underwent serious financial stress. One effect of this growing pressure on institutional budgets was to enhance, in the eyes of administrators, the value of the part-time teacher. No questions of tenure arose in such employment. Few if any benefits were extended. In some disciplines, notably English, part-timers with excellent qualifications were available for any teaching assignment, no matter how ill paid and ephemeral. Graduate schools continued through the 1970s to churn out Ph.D.s in the humanities and social sciences, long after the market for academic employment was saturated. Unable to find full-time academic employment as student enrollments and institutional budgets began to shrink, and unwilling to give up the long-treasured idea of a teaching career, they settled for part-time positions. In the scientific, professional, and technical fields, well-employed people were willing to teach part time for little money, if only because to do so confirmed their professional status.

With such cheaply gotten talent, four-year colleges and universities acquired some of the flexibility of the community colleges. They could quickly mount new programs and update established ones to satisfy students' new career interests, while limiting the involvement of expensive regular faculty (Keller 1983, pp. 23–24). Administrators could provide competent instruction by part-timers at between 50 and 80 percent of the direct cost of comparable instruction by full-time faculty (Lombardi 1976; Yang and Zak 1981). Because 80 percent of the operating budget of a typical institution of higher education is absorbed by personnel costs and because financial stringency is likely to continue at most institutions for the foreseeable future, the use of part-time faculty is likely to increase. Part-timers meaningfully conserve institutional dollars at all times. Moreover, they constitute a valuable source of contingent labor in periods of unstable enrollments and shifting program demand (Leslie, Kellams, and Gunne 1982; Lombardi 1975; McCabe and Brezner 1978).

Part-time Faculty Defined
No uniform definition of part-time faculty exists. The U.S. Department of Labor defines "part-time" as fewer than 35 hours of work in a given week, which suggests, for example, that 18 hours would constitute half time. In higher education, however, a full-time faculty member works close to 50 hours per week (Leslie 1978b, p. 1). Thus, the Department of Labor definition cannot be applied to higher education except in the most general way.

A second method for defining part-time faculty is by the number of credit hours taught. If a faculty member teaches fewer than the number of credit hours assigned to full-time faculty, the individual is characterized as part time. But teaching loads often vary from program to program and according to faculty members' rank. So this definition virtually precludes comparing part-time faculty across institutions or even among programs within institutions.

A third way to distinguish part-time faculty is provided by collective bargaining agreements or state statutes. Court decisions and collective bargaining are forcing colleges and universities to define part-time status more precisely and to clarify their policies regarding the employment status of various classes of faculty (Lombardi 1975). Some states, California for one, define part-time and full-time faculty by statute. In other states, many institutions provide no formal definitions, and the status of faculty is specified in individual teaching contracts. At larger institutions, the definition of part-time status varies across programs. For example, divisions of continuing education, evening programs, and off-campus instruction, where virtually all faculty are considered part time, can define part-time status differently. And the definition of part time can vary according to job-related and motivational characteristics of part-timers themselves.

For present purposes, "part-time faculty" is defined as anyone who (1) teaches less than the average full-time teaching load, or (2) has less than a full-time faculty assignment and range of duties, or (3) may have a temporary full-time assignment. The third category is included because the time base of temporary (and usually part-time) faculty appointments shifts according to institutional need or available funding: They may work full time one semester and part time the next. Further, some who technically meet the definition of full-time faculty may have pieced together a full-time workload by teaching part time at two or more institutions. All persons included in this definition of part-time faculty are nontenured and nonpermanent and have little or no job security unless specific mention is made of tenure status. The definition excludes full-time faculty or staff who are teaching an overload and graduate assistants who are teaching part time in the department where they are also pursuing a graduate degree.

Limitations on Information

The difficulty with definitions inevitably limits the amount and usefulness of information about part-time faculty that can be gleaned from the available data. Different institutions include in their categories of part-time faculty a variety of people performing a wide range of functions. Some institutional data include faculty in adult education, evening programs, off-campus instruction, and noncredit programs. Other data do not. The inability to separate full-time faculty who teach overloads from regular part-time faculty contributes to the problem. The fact that part-timers may teach at two or more institutions, and thus be counted twice, further confuses matters. Some data are collected at different times of the year. From the national perspective, the result is chaotic inconsistency. To achieve comparable data across institutions, national agreement is needed regarding what data to collect about whom, and when.

As of 1976, the only reasonably accurate information about part-time faculty came from surveys conducted by the American Council on Education in 1968–69 and again in 1972–73 (Cartter 1976). Since then, two national surveys of part-time faculty have been conducted—in 1976 by Tuckman and associates and in 1978 by Leslie and associates. The results of these surveys have been reported over and over again in numerous publications, but no studies of comparable scope have been conducted since. Little is known about part-time faculty from a national perspective (Leslie, Kellams, and Gunne 1982, p. 15).

Some statewide surveys of the status of part-time faculty have been made, including studies in Ohio, Maryland, and California. But statewide surveys cannot be compared or generalized to the total population because states' definitions and data-collection procedures vary widely.

In the community college sector, where the majority of part-time faculty are employed, a great deal of analysis and commentary is available about part-time faculty members' status, salaries, working conditions, educational and employment backgrounds, and development. This information, however, is useful primarily to faculty and administrators at community colleges and to researchers concentrating on two-year institutions (Eliason 1980, p. 6).

Less information is available on the use of part-time teachers in four-year colleges and almost none about their employment in universities.

The National Center for Education Statistics, for example, has not collected any statistics about part-time faculty since 1976, and they are summarized in the *Digest of Education Statistics, 1980*. Changes in definitions and methods of estimation NCES uses have led to wide variations in that agency's reporting of trends. The Equal Employment Opportunity Commission (EEOC) has not compiled or published any of the data on part-time faculty collected from EEO-6 reports. The last year for which EEOC has available aggregated data that include part-time faculty is 1977, although data about part-time faculty for 1981 were being processed in early 1984. The National Science Foundation's studies of faculty exclude those in the humanities and the professions, where the use of part-timers is heaviest (Leslie, Kellams, and Gunne 1982, p. 15). The American Association of University Professors continues to prepare an annual report on faculty salaries for full-time faculty, but it has not studied part-time faculty since Tuckman's work in 1976. The *Chronicle of Higher Education* last published substantive findings about part-time faculty in 1982.

The quality and quantity of information available certainly has not improved since 1982:

Lacking hard information and a clear sense of common practice, various interest groups have raised important questions regarding the part-time appointment. Administrators wonder if they can economize and hedge on long-term personnel commitments by relying increasingly on part-timers. Full-time faculty and their organizations worry about their waning power implied by use of a more temporary work force. Quality control is a focus of concern for all sides. And the swelling ranks of part-time faculty express anger and frustration over their treatment as outsiders. Looking to courts, legislators, labor boards, and accrediting bodies for resolution of the most difficult issues has proved futile. There are, indeed, no answers, little objective data, and an inability to define the basic questions. In such a chaotic environ-

ment, interest groups offer arguments and jockey for positions, but they do so in an informational vacuum (Leslie, Kellams, and Gunne 1982, pp. 1–2).

Invisibility and Myth

Some recent authors view personnel policy as applying to the permanent, core faculty. Part-time faculty are not identified as an important factor in retrenchment, and making greater use of them is an option only touched upon. While it is acknowledged that part-time faculty can provide expertise in specific curricular areas, often at a proportionally lower cost than full-time faculty and without long-term commitment, the predominant attitude is that the term "faculty" means full-time tenured faculty or faculty on the tenure track. Part-time faculty are as invisible in the literature as they are in the faculty club, and attitudinal barriers work to rob the part-timer of professional visibility:

> *At the opening faculty breakfast . . . a public university of moderate size in the west provided a list of new faculty members. Of the 40 names, 32 were listed as lecturers, adjunct, or visiting [faculty]. . . . Despite an hour and a half of speeches by the President, Chairman of the Faculty Senate and others, the high proportion of nomads was not mentioned in passing* (Furniss 1981, p. 97).

Myth and bias about part-timers are rife. Hiring part-time faculty, in the general view, is at the expense of program quality; the major advantage in hiring them is financial. When part-time faculty are discussed at all, it is primarily with respect to their disadvantages, not their advantages. Part-time faculty are seen as less well qualified, but studies comparing the effectiveness of part-time and full-time teaching are not cited. The prevailing attitude seems to be that part-time faculty should be "employed at lower compensation because [they have] less experience and preparation and [they should] receive fewer or no fringe benefits on the grounds that part-time faculty would typically be employed full-time elsewhere" (Mayhew 1979, p. 245).

It hardly seems necessary to observe that more careful, more comprehensive studies of part-time teaching in higher education are badly needed. Some (for example, Eliason 1980) recommend that data on part-timers be collected nationally, by institutional type; others (for example, Maher and Ebben 1978) focus their attention on collecting information about part-timers at the institutional level only. Part-time faculty have long been an integral part of the enterprise and surely will remain so. The pretense that they are a fringe group of stateless academics, marginal in capacity and thus exploitable without qualm, is grounded in what may fairly be called calculated ignorance. Federal agencies certainly should be under pressure to regularly collect, compile, and publish data on part-timers that would help support institutional research and independent investigations. The research community might exert more pressure for better and more timely data if institutional and state-level decision makers made it clear that information about part-time faculty was really wanted. But in fact, with few exceptions, part-timers still are regarded with neglected complacency in higher education. Like servants on the baronial estates of yesteryear, they are barely seen and hardly heard by their masters, and presumed to have no ears.

THE NATIONAL PROFILE OF
PART-TIME FACULTY

National Data

Despite the uneven quality and poor comparability of available statistics, a reasonably accurate assessment of the number and proportion of part-time faculty in the late 1970s is possible (see table 1). NCES compiles statistics about faculty in two categories: "faculty at the rank of instructor or above," and "all faculty," including "junior instructors." The latter are defined as assistant instructors, teaching fellows, and teaching and laboratory assistants; presumably, graduate teaching assistants are also included. With junior instructors deleted, the numbers of full- and part-time faculty NCES reported for 1975 and 1976 (the last years for which the agency published actual rather than estimated data) are very similar to the reports from other sources of data shown in table 1. The national total of full-time faculty ranges from 434,000 to 450,000, with a mean of 441,000. The number of part-time faculty ranges from 188,000 to 225,000, with a mean of 206,000. If the two means are accepted as roughly accurate, the total number of faculty in 1975 and 1976 was 647,000, of which 32 percent were part time. The NCES data indicate that, between 1975 (estimated) and 1976 (actual), the number of full-time faculty declined 1 percent while the number of part-time faculty increased 6 percent.

EEOC data from the EEO-6 forms provided by virtually all institutions are reported by tenure status. They show only 7 percent of all part-time faculty are tenured or are eligible for tenure. The EEOC data show that the total number of full-time faculty in the nation increased 4 percent from 1975 to 1977 and that part-time faculty increased 10 percent in the same period. As a result, the proportion of part-time faculty, which stood at 33 percent in 1975, rose to 34 percent in 1977.

Table 2 shows the estimated full-time equivalent (FTE) instructional faculty from 1970 to 1990.[1] Total FTE faculty increased an estimated 38 percent (451,000 to 624,000) between 1970 and 1980. FTE students increased 30 percent during the same period, so the student-faculty ratio improved, on a national basis at least, during the decade

---

[1]NCES made three alternative projections: low, intermediate, and high. Only the intermediate alternative for 1985 and 1990 is shown in tables 2 and 3.

TABLE 1
COMPARISON OF THE NUMBER AND PROPORTION OF
PART-TIME AND FULL-TIME FACULTY, REAL AND ESTIMATED

Source of Data	Full-time Faculty		Part-time Faculty		Total	
	Number (000)	Percent	Number (000)	Percent	Number (000)	Percent
1975 NCES: *Projection of Education Statistics to 1990–91*, table 22; *Digest of Education Statistics, 1980*, pp. 88–89.						
Junior instructors deleted[a]	440	70	188	30	628	100
Junior instructors included[a]	462	59	319	41	781	100
EEOC: All faculty reported on form EEO-6 (counted)[b]	439	67	212	33	651	100
Tenured and tenure-track faculty reported on form EEO-6 (counted)[b]	363	93	27	7	390	100
Non-tenure-track (extrapolated)	76	29	185	71	261	100
1976 NCES: Same sources as for 1975 (actual)						
Junior instructors deleted[a]	434	69	199	31	633	100
Junior instructors included[a]	462	58	331	42	793	100
Tuckman: Data from AAUP-sponsored survey (sources combined)[b]	450	67	225	33	675	100
1977 EEOC: All faculty reported on form EEO-6 (counted)[c]	455	66	233	34	688	100

a"Junior instructors" include assistant instructors, teaching fellows, and teaching and laboratory assistants.
bLeslie, Kellams, and Gunne 1982, p. 20.
cPhotocopied data from the 1977 aggregated tabulations of EEO-6 reports.

TABLE 2
ESTIMATED FULL-TIME EQUIVALENT INSTRUCTIONAL FACULTY IN ALL INSTITUTIONS OF HIGHER EDUCATION

	Total FTE Faculty		Instructional Faculty—Instructor or Above				Instructional Faculty Including Junior Instructors			
	Number (000)	Percent Increase from 1970	Full-time (000)	Percent	FTE of Part-time (000)	Percent	Full-time (000)	Percent	FTE of Part-time (000)	Percent
1970	451	—	369	92	33	8	383	85	69	15
1976	584	29	434	87	67	13	462	79	122	21
1980[a]	624	38	466	87	71	13	496	79	128	21
1985 Projection[b]	606	34	453	87	70	13	481	79	125	21
1990 Projection[b]	589	31	441	87	68	13	468	79	121	21

[a]Estimated data.
[b]Intermediate alternative.

Source: NCES 1982, p. 89.

(NCES 1982, p. 77). In terms of FTE, the proportion of part-time faculty to total faculty in the 1970s was of course much lower than the proportion of actual faculty. But it increased more rapidly. When junior instructors are deleted, the proportion increases considerably over the decade, from 8 percent of the total FTE faculty to 13 percent. When junior instructors are included, the proportion rises from 15 percent to 21 percent.

The estimated 38 percent increase in total FTE faculty between 1970 and 1980 (table 2) compares with a 48 percent estimated increase in the total number of faculty (table 3). The total number of part-time faculty grew from 104,000 in 1970 to 212,000 in 1980, not counting junior instructors, and from 191,000 to 350,000, including junior instructors.

The NCES projections from 1980 to 1990 in tables 2 and 3 involve four major assumptions that are open to question:

1. The proportion of part-time faculty will remain constant.
2. The total FTE faculty will not be affected by an increase in the proportion of part-time faculty, should such an increase occur.
3. The demand for additional faculty will decline proportionately with any decline in FTE enrollments. (NCES and others acknowledge that when the numbers of faculty were projected, no one knew what would happen to enrollment during the 1980s.)
4. The replacement rate in successive years will be constant, amounting to 4.5 percent of the previous year for the low and intermediate projections and 6 percent of the previous year for the high projections. (Cartter (1976), on the other hand, used a replacement rate of 1.5 percent per year to project the demand for new faculty.)

NCES makes two other assumptions that are of less concern but can also be challenged—that institutions have begun to deny tenure at an increasing rate, forcing younger faculty out of the profession, and that the large number of faculty retirements in the 1970s will be equaled in the 1980s (NCES 1982, pp. 77–79). Others disagree with the first

TABLE 3
NUMBER AND PROPORTION OF PART-TIME AND FULL-TIME FACULTY, REAL AND ESTIMATED

	Total		Faculty—Instructor or Above				Faculty Including Junior Instructors			
	Number (000)	Percent Increase from 1970	Full-time (000)	Percent	Part-time (000)	Percent	Full-time (000)	Percent	Part-time (000)	Percent
1960	276	—	154	65	82	35	162	59	114	41
1970	573	—	369	78	104	22	383	67	191	33
1976	793	38	434	69	199	31	462	58	331	42
1980[a]	846	48	466	69	212	31	496	59	350	41
1985 Projection[b]	824	44	453	68	210	32	481	58	343	42
1990 Projection[b]	799	39	441	68	204	32	468	59	331	41

[a]Estimated data.
[b]Intermediate alternative.

Source: NCES 1980, p. 106; 1982, p. 88.

assumption (Atelsek and Gomberg 1980; Maryland State Board for Higher Education 1982), and several unknowns, including changes in the legislation and regulation of mandatory retirement, may undermine the second.

Although table 2 shows a 38 percent increase in total FTE faculty from 1970 to 1980, for the 1980s, NCES's intermediate projection shows a decline in the numbers of both full-time and part-time FTE faculty, whether or not junior instructors are included. The assumption that the ratio of full-time to part-time faculty will not change figures large in this projection. On table 3, the 1960s and 1970s displayed a pattern of steady growth for both full-time and part-time faculty, whether or not junior instructors are included. On the bases of both full-time equivalency and head count, total part-time faculty grew faster than full-time faculty from 1970 to 1980. And both tables predict declines for the 1980s. If one assumes that NCES's replacement rate is overly optimistic, an even greater decline is foreshadowed.

Total part-time faculty grew faster than full-time faculty from 1970 to 1980.

Academic Demand

In labor-market parlance, "academic demand" is the demand for new faculty at colleges and universities. The number of new faculty to be hired depends on four main factors: enrollment, student/faculty ratios, retirements, and net migration of experienced faculty. The first two factors affect the demand for expansion; the latter two determine the demand for replacement (Cartter 1976, p. 221). Other factors affect academic demand as well: the financial status of the institution and the growth or decline of interest in various disciplines.

What implications does academic demand have with respect to increased use of part-time faculty? Academic demand for faculty has many of the same characteristics as demand for investment goods in the economy as a whole. It is largely "derived" demand, depending on the rate of change in the total number of students attending college. If the ratio of students to faculty remains constant at 15 to 1, for example, and total enrollment of students climbs from 5,000,000 to 5,150,000, then 10,000 new faculty will be required to handle the additional students. As with investment goods, relatively small changes in the demand for the final product (the education of students) produce exaggerated changes in the demand for investment inputs (faculty). Fairly significant swings in the demand for new faculty must be expected because of its dependency upon enrollment (Cartter 1976, pp. 2–3). ("Faculty," as used by Cartter and others, means permanent faculty.)

Cartter's comprehensive assessment of the future demand for faculty was based on data from the early 1970s, which was later updated and extended by William Bowen and associates at Princeton (Tickton et al. 1982, pp. 183–87). These studies are compared here with NCES's projections. All sources agree that if patterns of college enrollment follow past trends and if the instructional process remains similar to the 1970s, the period from 1980 to 1995 will be a lean period for those seeking faculty positions.

Table 4 examines real and projected enrollment (the demand) in all institutions of higher education from 1970 to 1990. The period from 1970 to 1980 was characterized by steady growth, with an increase in total enrollment of 30 percent. The increase in total enrollment in two-year institutions was 71 percent. Undergraduate enrollment increased 15 percent in four-year institutions, and graduate enrollment increased 32 percent. (This increase in graduate enrollment must be viewed as a percentage of the total numbers of graduate students.) The projections for 1980 to 1990 are very different, ranging from −1 percent to 8 percent (low and intermediate alternatives, respectively) for two-year colleges and from −11 percent (low) to 7 percent (intermediate) for graduate enrollment. The greatest decline in enrollment, however, is projected for undergraduate four-year institutions: −20 percent (low) to −12 percent (intermediate). If actual enrollments fall within these projected ranges, demand for new faculty will be caused by factors other than increased enrollments (Cartter 1976; NCES 1982; Tickton et al. 1982).

Graduate schools expanded in the 1960s to meet the requirements of a rapidly growing research and education market (the supply). The high level of demand for new Ph.D.s established in the mid-1960s led to the increased production of doctorates in the 1970s and 1980s. NCES data (table 5) show that doctoral production totaled 118,000 from 1966 to 1970 and rose to 168,000 from 1971 to 1975. NCES's intermediate projection foresees little change in the level of doctoral production from 1980 to 1990.

TABLE 4
FULL-TIME EQUIVALENT ENROLLMENT IN ALL INSTITUTIONS OF HIGHER EDUCATION: 1970–1990

	Total		Undergraduate Two Year		Undergraduate Four Year		Graduate	
	Number (000)	Percent Increase from 1970	Number (000)	Percent Increase from 1970	Number (000)	Percent Increase from 1970	Number (000)	Percent Increase from 1970
1970	6,737	—	1,518	—	4,458	—	599	—
1975	8,481	26	2,579	70	4,914	10	756	26
1980	8,749	30	2,589	71	5,108	15	791	32
		Percent Increase from 1980		Percent Increase from 1980		Percent Increase from 1980		Percent Increase from 1980
1985 Projection[a]								
Low alternative	8,046	– 8	2,585	0	4,442	– 13	763	– 4
Intermediate alternative	8,620	– 2	2,742	6	4,700	– 8	871	10
1990 Projection[a]								
Low alternative	7,614	– 13	2,553	– 1	4,114	– 20	704	– 11
Intermediate alternative	8,428	– 4	2,782	8	4,488	– 12	846	7

[a]The high alternative projections are deemed unrealistic and are therefore not shown.

Source: NCES 1982. p. 58.

TABLE 5
ESTIMATED DEMAND FOR FTE FACULTY IN INSTITUTIONS OF HIGHER EDUCATION COMPARED WITH DOCTORAL PRODUCTION

Source of Data	Doctoral Production (000)	Demand for New Faculty		
		Replacement (000)	Growth (000)	Total (000)
1966–1970				
Cartter[a]	118	25.9	120.0	145.9
NCES				
1971–1975				
Cartter	168	28.8	37.9	66.7
NCES[a]		106.0 [35.3][b]	123.0	229.0 [158.3]
1976–1980				
Cartter	165	28.1	40.3	68.4
NCES		133.0 [44.3]	50.0	183.0 [94.3]
1981–1985				
Cartter		30.0	–8.4	21.6
NCES (projected)				
Low alternative	154	135.0 [45.0]	–59.0	76.0 [–14.0]
Intermediate alternative	167	143.0 [48.0]	–18.0	125.0 [30.0]
1986–1990				
Cartter		33.8	–11.9	21.9
NCES (projected)				
Low alternative	132	122.0 [40.0]	–34.0	88.0 [6.0]
Intermediate alternative	169	135.0 [45.0]	–17.0	118.0 [28.0]

[a]Cartter uses a 1.5 percent replacement rate and an assumed student/faculty ratio of 17:1 in all his projections; NCES uses a 4.5 percent replacement rate for its low and intermediate alternatives. The high alternative is not shown because it is based on a 6 percent replacement rate, which is deemed unrealistic.

[b]All numbers in brackets are NCES data adjusted for comparison with Cartter by using a 1.5 percent replacement rate. The different assumptions in projecting growth cannot be adjusted.

Sources: Cartter 1976, p. 123; NCES 1976, pp. 52–53 (for 1966–1970); NCES 1982, pp. 70, 90–91 (for 1971–1990).

Table 5 compares Cartter's projections of academic demand with later projections by NCES. The wide discrepancy in the data is reduced if Cartter's 1.5 percent replacement rate is used instead of NCES's 4.5 percent replacement rate. The high rate of growth in enrollment from 1966 to 1970 led to a total demand for 146,000 new faculty. For 1971 to 1980, Cartter estimated that the demand for new faculty would be 135,000, or 11,000 fewer than the total for the five previous years. NCES, in sharp contrast, estimated an increase of 73 percent, from 145,900 to 252,600, even when its projection is based on a 1.5 percent replacement rate.

By comparison, all projections for the 1980s are bleak indeed. NCES's low projection is that demand for new faculty during the 1980s will be only 40 percent of the demand in the 1970s. Cartter projected a demand of 43,500 positions, or 30 percent of his total for the seventies. William Bowen's update of Cartter's projection estimates a total of 100,000 academic positions' becoming available between 1980 and 1995. The Department of Labor forecasts a 15 percent decline in number of faculty between 1982 and 1995 (Evangelauf 1984).

It is virtually certain, then, that doctoral production during the 1980s will far exceed the demand for new faculty (Cartter 1976; Lewis 1980; NCES 1982; Tickton 1982). Because of the time involved in earning a Ph.D., most of those who will receive doctoral degrees during the 1980s are already in graduate school. Therefore, a severe imbalance in supply seems unavoidable. To further complicate matters, institutions do not feel a need to reduce graduate enrollment. Enrollment-driven academic budgets provide an incentive for public institutions to maintain a high level of graduate enrollments, and university departments with substantial undergraduate teaching responsibilities feel a need (warranted or not) for a continuing supply of inexpensive teaching assistants. As job placement is not the university's responsibility, it does not experience the economic sanctions imposed on business for overproduction (Cartter 1976, pp. 238–44).

Academic demand should be differentiated by field. In the humanities, for example, it is quite apparent that a significant oversupply of doctorates will exist for the next five to 10 years or beyond. In new fields like environmental biology, computer science, or business, surpluses are likely to be nonexistent. New Ph.D.s with specializations in romantic poetry or medieval history are likely to find few nonacademic alternatives where they can use their training. Economists specializing in international trade or finance and computer engineers, however, are well suited for a wide array of employment possibilities—and the opportunities outside academe are attractive. As a result, various studies show a substantial decline in the percentage of recent Ph.D.s on college and university faculties in a number of science and engineering fields (National Research Council 1979, p. 1). (A recent Ph.D. is one who has obtained a degree within the past seven years.) Factors other than lucrative job offers outside academe also contribute to this decline, however—slowdowns in the growth of enrollment in some scientific fields, a lessening of support for research, and low rates of retirement among present faculty. Radner and Kuh's study (National Research Council 1979) concluded that all these factors taken together could cause the annual academic demand for new science and engineering Ph.D.s to drop by nearly 50 percent between 1978 and 1985, with a further drop in the 1990s (p. 30).

When the supply of new Ph.D.s outstrips the demand, it has personal and organizational consequences:

The odds are against the new but unplaced Ph.D. becoming productive in some kind of non-academic holding pattern. Knowledge production involves much more than individualistic development of an idea. It depends on effective interaction among creative minds. One must work within the network of scholars who are actively producing in order to be productive oneself. . . .

Furthermore, if the recent Ph.D. has not been academically employed for a few years, he or she may be ignored by hiring institutions. Newly minted Ph.D.'s will likely prove more attractive than those who have slipped into academic dormancy. . . .

Last, but certainly not least in importance, we must have a deep and genuine concern for the crushing personal tragedies that result when those who desire an intellectually active career do not have the opportunity to try it. The average Ph.D. age is about 30. . . . Begin-

*ning at age five, the attainment of that degree represents
an exceptionally large number of years of schooling. To
persevere in advanced education for that long means
that the student must have an intense desire to be a college and university teacher. The exit from the scholarly
tracks must have devastating psychological and health
consequences for the derailed individuals* (Blackburn
1978, pp. 102–3).

Most students of academic demand view it from the
perspective of the full-time traditional career (Cartter 1976;
NCES 1982; Tickton 1982). Thus, they must be pessimis-
tic. A more hopeful outlook is possible, however, based on
the steady increase in the numbers of people employed as
part-time faculty. With the decline in the availability of
full-time, tenure-track faculty positions, many new Ph.D.s
will seek other careers, but this situation does not necessarily exclude them from the scholarly life. They may
make scholarly contributions through employment in industry or government. They may teach part time, to gain
personal satisfaction. Some may piece together several
part-time positions into a full-time faculty career. Ph.D.s in
different disciplines will find widely varying answers to the
decreased availability of tenure positions.

If this hypothesis that new Ph.D.s will want to affiliate in
some way with higher education proves correct, the result
could be the improved quality of academic programs
through the use of a greater number of Ph.D.s as part-time
faculty, who bring to their teaching and research their educational credentials and their experience outside academe.
The projected bleak period from 1980 to 1995 for traditional faculty hiring may in fact be an opportunity for
higher education to increase its use of part-time faculty.
Although this hypothesis has its pitfalls and counter-
arguments, a viable—even desirable—alternative to tenured positions in unstable and financially difficult times
may be to increase part-time faculty appointments.

CHARACTERISTICS OF
PART-TIME FACULTY

The usefulness of the national profile of part-time faculty in the preceding chapter is limited in two principal ways. First, available national data are inadequate and out of date. Second, highly aggregated statistics do not reveal what sorts of people are teaching part time, why they teach, in what types of institutions, and under what conditions. This chapter addresses that second limitation, describing part-timers insofar as existing information will allow.

An observation about part-timers in community colleges in the 1970s is still pertinent:

> *It is important to obtain information about the background, motivation, and aspiration of part-time teachers because community college administrators frequently justify their discriminatory treatment of this faculty in two ways: First, they claim that part-time instructors lack a substantial commitment to the institution. Second, they assert these teachers do not need larger salaries. After all, the recurrent argument goes, the typical part-time teacher is a real-estate agent salesman who stops off at the college one night for the enjoyment of sharing his expertise with a few students. Underlying this statement are the assumptions that the average part-time faculty member is a man, that he invests virtually no time in class preparation, that he lacks the qualifications for a regular faculty appointment, that he holds a full-time job elsewhere, that he does not regard himself primarily as an educator, and that he is satisfied with his salary and working conditions* (Abel 1976, p. 4).

Three basic realities pertain to part-time faculty. First, they are not alike in their reasons for seeking part-time employment, their faculty roles, or their career aspirations. Second, the reasons for employing part-time faculty differ from one institution to another. And third, part-time employment in academe differs in character from that in other settings. Therefore, classifying or characterizing part-time faculty is difficult (Emmet 1981, p. 1). This chapter describes part-time faculty according to their distribution by type of institution and discipline, their individual characteristics (including demographics, work history, and career aspirations), and the types of employment they find.

The Distribution of Part-timers

Of all part-time faculty in higher education, 53 percent are employed in two-year colleges (Eliason 1980, p. 2; Tuckman 1978, p. 313). In 1968–69, there were 36,420 part-time faculty, or one for every 2.6 full-time faculty, in the community colleges. By 1975–76, there were 110,976 part-time faculty, or one for every 1.8 full-time faculty members (Tuckman and Vogler 1978, p. 70). Based on numbers, many community colleges employ more part-time than full-time faculty (Leslie, Kellams, and Gunne 1982; Maher and Ebben 1978). The community college neither needs nor can afford to invest heavily in permanent faculty whose specializations interest only a thinly spread national constituency. Community colleges must meet strictly local demand for courses and programs of immediate interest, either with or without credit, taught on campus or off campus.

In California in 1974–75, for example, 40 percent more people were employed part time than full time in the community colleges. In terms of full-time equivalency, part-timers filled 28 percent of the regular teaching positions in community colleges. They were most numerous in such programs as business, management, public affairs, home economics, computer and information science, and law (Fryer 1977, p. 14). The programs with the greatest number of part-time faculty usually were vocational or technical or were those in which the least number of individuals qualified for full-time faculty positions were available, such as health technology or data processing (Eliason 1980, p. 4).

Use of part-time faculty correlates substantially with enrollment of part-time students. Many such students want short-term courses designed to impart specific skills rather than courses offered in a degree program. Typically, community colleges offer such courses in evening or off-campus instructional programs, and they are taught by part-timers (Leslie 1978a; Leslie, Kellams, and Gunne 1982, pp. 3–4). Academic programs requiring more continuity in instruction and more investment of time by students and faculty rely more heavily on full-time faculty. A study of the use of part-time faculty in community colleges by region showed that the average community college used 88 percent more part-time faculty in 1977 than it did in 1973 but only 1 percent more full-time faculty. The average number of faculty per institution increased 36 percent,

The community college neither needs nor can afford to invest heavily in permanent faculty.

while enrollment increased 28 percent. Enrollment of full-time students rose only 1 percent, while enrollment of part-time students rose 44 percent (Guthrie-Morse 1979).

Thirty-four percent of the part-timers in higher education are located in four-year institutions (Tuckman 1978, p. 313). The proportion of part-time to full-time faculty at four-year institutions grew from a ratio of 1 to every 3.6 full-time faculty in 1972–73 to 1 to every 2.8 in 1976–77 (Tuckman and Vogler 1978, p. 70).

In private schools with enrollment under 1,000, little or no endowment, and a regional reputation at best, the flexibility and savings in costs that result from the use of part-time faculty are irresistible. Many of these institutions are in straitened circumstances and cannot maintain high ratios of full-time to part-time faculty. The selection of part-time faculty is critical, however. When part-time faculty roughly equal full-timers in number and constitute 10 to 15 percent of the college's FTE faculty, their performance in the classroom may tip the institution toward excellence or mediocrity (Maher and Ebben 1978, p. 75).

Universities employ 13 percent of the part-time faculty in higher education (Tuckman 1978, p. 313). Unlike community colleges and small private schools, nationally respected research universities find a number of disincentives for relying on part-timers. Generally they use graduate teaching assistants instead of part-time faculty (Fink 1976–77). They deliberately hold the number of part-time faculty down or work to decrease the number employed (Leslie, Kellams, and Gunne 1982, p. 28). Exceptions to this generalization are large urban universities, which can staff many programs because of the concentration of talent in metropolitan areas. These institutions rely heavily on part-timers in certain fields and for certain functions. The performing arts, for example, have historically used part-time faculty. Across all universities, the proportion of part-time to full-time faculty has grown from 1 part-time to 4.5 full-time faculty in 1972–73 to 1 to 3.8 in 1976–77 (Leslie, Kellams, and Gunne 1982, pp. 28–29; Tuckman and Vogler 1978, p. 70).

As states become more concerned about the cost of supporting public higher education and the need for state-level coordination of academic programs, they are paying increased attention to part-time faculty. In 1979, a state study in Missouri determined that 23.7 percent of the total instructional faculty was part-time. These faculty were concentrated in computer and information sciences, business, data processing, engineering, and public services. Seventy-seven percent of the part-time faculty in Missouri's state institutions were in two-year colleges, 21 percent were in four-year colleges, and 2 percent were employed by the University of Missouri. The Missouri study raised questions about the possibly excessive use of part-time faculty in some disciplines (St. John 1979). A similar study by the Maryland State Board for Higher Education (1982) found that between 1975 and 1981, full-time instructional faculty increased 1.5 percent, and part-time faculty increased 74 percent. Community colleges accounted for the highest percentage of part-time faculty, the University of Maryland the lowest.

Why does the use of part-time faculty vary so much among colleges and universities? Institutions use part-time faculty for numerous reasons, and they can be increasing employment of part-timers in some programs while decreasing it in others at the same time for different reasons. Strong institutional reasoning is behind the decisions to increase or decrease the use of part-time faculty, and institutions that make such decisions may be characterized as "adapting" or "retrenching" (Leslie, Kellams, and Gunne 1982).

Adapting institutions are characterized by a heavily tenured faculty in traditional fields and a weak market position. They have neither a geographic appeal nor the prestige of highly selective private institutions. They are seriously affected by the demographic factors characterizing the 1980s and are acutely sensitive to students' interests. Without information about the durability of such interests and with the need to maintain enrollment, the institutions cannot confidently judge the need for investment in full-time faculty. Therefore, they hire part-timers to staff new programs and new courses aimed at maintaining enrollment.

Retrenching institutions suffer intense budget problems, caused by a sometimes complex mix of conditions. Tuition and subsidies will not support either increases in or maintenance of the number of faculty positions. Part-timers can be hired for less money than the full-timers who retire or vacate positions. They keep down faculty costs over time because their salaries increase more slowly than those of full-time faculty, if at all. With careful planning and judicious use of part-time faculty, retrenching institutions can live within their budget constraints. When the institutions must cut back, part-timers can be terminated easily; they seldom have contractual security (Leslie, Kellams, and Gunne 1982, pp. 28–30).

The academic profile of many institutions is being converted—sometimes slowly, sometimes rapidly—as the mix of faculty changes and the mix of programs is altered. The cloistered, residential undergraduate college offers the new adult learner a variety of nondegree programs; the community college develops training programs for workers in a particular industry; the university synthesizes two fields of study, fuses them with a clinical component, and offers a new degree. In all cases, the use of part-time faculty can contribute significantly to adaptability by permitting access to needed expertise while avoiding permanency and inflexibility (Leslie, Kellams, and Gunne 1982, p. 32).

The Tuckman Taxonomy

The results of a survey in 1976 by Howard Tuckman and associates, under the sponsorship of the American Association of University Professors (AAUP), provides the foundation for the following discussion of the characteristics of part-time faculty.[2] As of this writing, the taxonomy developed from that survey is the only extant analysis of data from a large national sample that depicts variation in the population of part-time faculty. In fact, no other study on any scale probes so extensively the differences among part-time faculty. The differences Tuckman found may have changed in recent years in response to various influences, such as tighter institutional budgets and the women's movement. Nonetheless, the survey yielded still-

[2]A random stratified sample of institutions was surveyed, including private and public schools with various levels of degree programs in different regions of the country and with different numbers of full- and part-time faculty. The researchers sent questionnaires to the schools to be distributed to all part-time faculty on their payrolls in the spring of 1976. They distributed 10,000 questionnaires; 3,763 were returned to the AAUP from part-timers at 128 academic institutions (see Tuckman, Caldwell, and Vogler 1978).

valuable data about demographics, career aspirations, work history, and types of employment.

Tuckman's analysis of the reasons that part-timers choose such employment produced seven mutually exclusive categories:

- The **semiretireds** constituted the most homogeneous group of part-timers. This category was restricted to former full-time academics who scaled down to part-time work, former full-timers outside of academe who were semiretired, or those who had taught part time during their entire career. The semiretireds taught fewer hours and were less concerned about future job prospects than were the part-timers in the other categories.
- The **students** were usually employed as part-timers in institutions other than the one where they were pursuing a graduate degree. (The category did not include graduate assistants teaching in the same department and same institution where they were pursuing a degree.) They were likely to be teaching to gain experience and to augment income. They were also likely to be geographically immobile while finishing the degree. Like semiretireds, they did not see their future as being tied to their current employer.
- The **hopeful full-timers** were those who could not find full-time academic positions. They included those with no prior faculty employment who were gathering experience to augment their case for becoming a full-time employee, those with prior experience who were working part time but would prefer a full-time position, and those working enough part-time hours at one or more schools to constitute full-time employment but under several contracts, each providing only part-time status. These people were flexible as to the hours they worked, highly concerned about their careers, and willing to be mobile.
- The **full-mooners** were individuals who held another, primary job of at least 35 hours a week. Their part-time income amounted to only a small part of their total earnings, and usually their part-time employment only supplemented their full-time career. They spent relatively little time preparing lectures and other

teaching activities, and they limited the number of hours they taught. This heterogeneous group consisted of people with a wide range of educational backgrounds, experience, and work histories. The full-mooners included full-time tenured faculty teaching overload courses.

- The **homeworkers** worked part-time because they cared for children or other relatives. Responsibilities at home limited the number of hours they could work. Part-time employment might be the sole source of support for the homeworker's household, or it might supplement the income of a spouse or other family member. The homeworker was assumed to be geographically immobile.
- The **part-mooners** consisted of people working part time in one academic institution while holding a second job of under 35 hours a week elsewhere. Part-time faculty fell into this category for one or more of several reasons: The other employer did not provide the opportunity to work more hours, making two jobs necessary to obtain the desired income; the person held two jobs to gain psychic rewards not obtainable from one job alone; concerned about future employment, the person was hedging by developing working contacts in several places; the person's skills were highly specialized and could be used to only a limited extent by a single employer.
- The **part-unknowners** consisted of part-time faculty whose reasons for working part-time were either unknown, transitory, or highly subjective. This mixed bag included persons with a high preference for leisure or recreational activity over work, those in transition between jobs, those who work part time primarily to stay in touch with the academic world, and others with motives that the analysis failed to capture (Tuckman 1978, pp. 307–13).

The Tuckman taxonomy is summarized in table 6. Full-mooners and students accounted for nearly half of the total part-time faculty in the sample. Hopeful full-timers and part-mooners, who overlap somewhat, constituted almost one-third of the sample. Semiretireds and homeworkers amounted to less than 10 percent of the total.

TABLE 6
TAXONOMY OF PART-TIME FACULTY
BY NUMBER AND PERCENTAGE IN SAMPLE

Category	Percentage of Total	Number in Sample
Semiretired	2.8	107
Student	21.2	796
Hopeful full-timer	16.6	624
Full-mooner	27.6	1,039
Homeworker	6.4	240
Part-mooner	13.6	512
Part-unknowner	11.8	445
Total	100.0	3,763

Source: Tuckman 1978, p. 308.

Demographic Characteristics of Part-time Faculty

Tuckman's demographic information about the different categories of part-timers was accurate at the time of his study. Where available, Tuckman's data are supplemented by information from other studies; however, little information is available that is more current. The demographic characteristics of part-time faculty identified by Tuckman are summarized in table 7.

According to the table, most part-timers in 1976 were between 35 and 45 years old, with an average age of 40. (While two contemporaneous studies (Grymes 1976 and Quanty 1976) put the average age of part-time faculty at about 33, these studies were limited to part-time faculty at only two community colleges.) Tuckman found that almost 39 percent of all part-time faculty were women but that their distribution among categories varied widely. Other than the homeworkers, the highest percentages of women were hopeful full-timers and students. Just as substantial numbers of women were completing doctoral programs and entering the labor force as hopeful full-timers (probably the

TABLE 7
SELECTED CHARACTERISTICS OF PART-TIME FACULTY: DEMOGRAPHIC INFORMATION

	Semi-retired	Student	Hopeful Full-timer	Full-mooner	Home-worker	Part-mooner	Part-unknowner	All Part-timers
Demographic								
Average age	62.3	35.1	37.6	41.3	36.1	41.2	44.4	40.0
Percent female	25.2	48.5	52.6	14.1	96.7	31.6	39.3	38.7
Percent black	3.7	3.3	2.1	3.1	0.8	3.5	4.5	3.1
Percent Caucasian	94.4	88.8	91.3	93.0	97.1	91.6	90.6	91.7
Percent other minority	1.9	7.9	6.6	3.9	2.1	4.9	4.9	5.2
Percent married	77.6	66.8	66.8	84.1	96.7	74.3	81.6	76.5
Percent with spouse in academe	5.3	13.6	19.7	7.8	30.1	11.1	15.2	13.7
Percent with resident children	23.4	51.5	49.4	68.3	98.3	55.9	53.7	58.8
Total own earned income in 1976	$11,703	$10,463	$ 8,660	$22,802	$ 5,346	$17,268	$15,957	$14,826
Total household income in 1976	22,883	18,454	18,555	27,990	26,161	24,861	25,361	23,410
Percent own earned income of household income	51.0	57.0	47.0	81.0	20.0	69.0	63.0	63.0
Educational								
Percent with Ph.D.	31.4	3.9	30.3	21.1	15.8	23.8	24.9	19.7
Percent with M.A.[a]	41.9	56.0	56.8	46.4	55.0	44.6	40.0	49.7
Scholarly								
Percent who have published an article	26.2	15.5	23.6	20.4	12.9	20.3	20.0	19.5
Average number of articles published	2.9	0.5	1.2	1.3	0.4	1.2	1.2	1.1
Experiential								
Percent previously full-time	49.5	25.6	40.7	20.5	30.4	29.1	31.9	28.9
Average years taught full-time	12.5	1.4	2.2	1.9	1.5	2.8	3.9	2.5
Average years taught part-time	6.1	3.4	4.0	5.1	4.4	5.2	5.0	4.6

[a]Includes M.A., professional or specialist diploma, and those who have completed all requirements but the dissertation for a doctoral degree.

Source: Tuckman 1978, p. 309.

result of affirmative action efforts during the 1970s), the number of available full-time positions began decreasing. Along with their male colleagues, these women found that the only employment available was as part-time faculty (Leslie 1978a; Stern et al. 1981; Yang and Zak 1981). Studies of the distribution of men and women among part-time faculty in three different community colleges showed that the proportion who were women ranged from 32 percent to 53 percent (Abel 1976; Grymes 1976; Quanty 1976).

Three-fourths of the part-time faculty in Tuckman's study were married, but only 14 percent had a spouse who was also employed in higher education. Thirty percent of the homeworkers and 20 percent of the hopeful full-timers, however, had spouses so employed. In those two categories, the part-timers earned the smallest share of total household income. Tuckman's published data do not allow examination of marital status, child-rearing status, and earned income by sex, and the problems of dual-career couples in academe are of marginal concern here. Tuckman's data regarding marital status and career of spouse, however, appear to substantiate a more recent study of the difficulties couples encounter when seeking academic employment for both spouses in geographical proximity (Gappa, O'Barr, and St. John-Parsons 1980).

The percentage of part-time faculty in 1976 who were Caucasian was above 90 percent across all categories except students, where it was just under 90 percent. Grymes (1976) and Quanty (1976) substantiate Tuckman's data, but the effect of affirmative action programs may well have significantly altered this situation in the 1980s.

Tuckman found that just under 70 percent of the part-time faculty held an advanced degree, approximately 50 percent held at least a master's degree, and some 20 percent held a doctorate. The largest percentage (over 30 percent) who had doctoral degrees was in the semiretireds and the hopeful full-timers. The percentage of part-time faculty with a doctorate varied by institutional type (Tuckman 1981, p. 9). In four-year institutions, for example, 35.9 percent of the male and 21.3 percent of the female part-time faculty had doctorates. In universities, the proportions were 45.5 percent of the men and 24.6 percent of the women. Other findings are similar. In Ohio, the percentage holding the doctorate among part-time faculty was highest at state universities (32 percent) and lowest at community colleges (12 percent) (Yang and Zak 1981, p. 16). Based on national data, 75 percent of two-year college faculty have a master's degree and nearly 14 percent have a doctorate. The percentage with doctorates is likely to rise during the 1980s, partially because fewer full-time positions will be available (Eliason 1980, p. 9). In a study limited to private junior colleges, 86 percent of the responding institutions reported that part-time faculty had levels of formal education equal to that of full-time faculty (Smith 1981). In two other studies, each analyzing a single community college, 50 percent to 55 percent of the part-time faculty had a master's degree, and 8 percent to 14 percent had a doctoral degree (Grymes 1976; Quanty 1976).

Tuckman also found that 20 percent of part-time faculty had published an article and that the average number of articles published was slightly over one. Yang and Zak (1981) found that 30 percent of the part-time faculty in their study had published at least one article and that 35 percent had presented at least one paper at a professional meeting. Part-timers at state universities were significantly more productive in both respects than those at private institutions or community colleges (p. 16).

Educational preparation and scholarly activity cannot be viewed as the only indicators of quality in the comparison of part-time to regular full-time faculty. Part-time faculty represent a wide range of skills, experience, and expertise. Those who hold full-time positions elsewhere may have expertise that enriches their teaching as much as scholarly accomplishment would. Accomplished performers, for example, frequently teach instrumental music. Part-timers frequently teach accounting, business law, economics, and public administration quite ably. And mutual benefits accrue; real-world professionals usually find that teaching at a college or university can be an important personal stimulus and a way of keeping up in their fields (Leslie, Kellams, and Gunne 1982; Tuckman 1978, 1981).

Career Aspirations and Experience
Tuckman's determinations about why part-timers teach, what kinds of careers they seek, and their work experience are shown in table 8. The most striking finding was that

TABLE 8
SELECTED CHARACTERISTICS OF PART-TIME FACULTY: CAREER ASPIRATIONS AND WORK HISTORY

	Semi-retired	Student	Hopeful Full-timer	Full-mooner	Home-worker	Part-mooner	Part-unknowner	All Part-timers
Job mobility; career aspirations								
Percent that sought a full-time academic position[a]	8.6	26.8	62.5	6.9	5.4	10.7	11.0	21.4
Percent that sought a nonacademic position[a]	6.6	18.0	33.0	7.6	2.5	11.3	8.1	14.3
Percent that don't want a full-time position	45.3	7.9	0.8	18.2	23.6	16.6	23.3	14.4
Percent free to move	39.6	61.6	65.6	39.9	20.7	42.2	36.5	47.8
Percent unwilling to move	15.1	30.5	33.5	42.0	55.7	41.2	40.2	37.9
Percent that received an academic offer[b]	44.4	30.8	12.7	84.5	100.0	85.2	48.9	32.8
Percent that received a nonacademic offer[b]	85.7	84.4	40.9	137.2	283.3	122.8	100.0	82.9
Work history								
Average months worked in last 12	7.6	8.1	8.7	7.6	8.5	7.6	8.0	8.0
Average years worked in last 10	6.6	4.2	5.2	5.2	5.2	5.0	5.1	5.0
Average years did not work at all	2.2	0.7	1.1	0.8	2.9	1.0	1.8	1.1

[a]Number seeking a full-time job divided by total number in category.
[b]Number that received an offer divided by number who sought a full-time position.

Source: Tuckman 1978, pp. 311, 313.

62.5 percent of the hopeful full-timers had actively sought full-time academic work, but only 12.7 percent of the seekers had received an offer. By contrast, 21.4 percent of part-time faculty as a whole had sought full-time faculty work, and 32.8 percent of them had gotten an offer. The hopeful full-timers fared no better, comparatively, on the non-academic job market. Thirty-three percent had sought full-time nonacademic positions, but only 40.9 percent of the seekers had received offers. Among all part-timers, only 14.3 percent had looked for full-time nonacademic work, and 82.9 percent of them got offers.

Career aspirations do not always correspond with mobility. For example, while virtually all the hopeful full-timers wanted a position, only two-thirds of them were free to move. Across all categories of part-timers, almost half indicated they were free to move. Yet those who responded that they were the least willing to move (full-mooners, homeworkers, part-mooners, and part-unknowners) had the highest percentage of nonacademic and academic offers. Perhaps their focus on the local job market contributed to their success.

Tuckman's data on work history of part-time faculty indicate unusual stability across categories. In most categories, part-time faculty had worked for about five of the last 10 years. Despite the differing career aspirations across Tuckman's categories, part-time faculty showed few differences in work history. Only those part-time faculty having some continuity of employment may have chosen to respond to Tuckman's questionnaire, however.

Many part-time faculty, particularly those who teach at community colleges, are employed in one or more other positions. A statewide survey of part-time faculty found that 27.3 percent of the part-time faculty employed in California community colleges were actually full-time faculty teaching an overload course, usually in the evening. Another 23 percent were employed full-time in business or industry, 11.5 percent were elementary and secondary school teachers, and 9 percent were employed at public agencies (Sewell, Brydon, and Plosser 1976, pp. 8–9). Other studies substantiate these findings (Abel 1976; Grymes 1976; Quanty 1976). Yang and Zak's survey (1981) of part-time faculty in Ohio shows a similar distribution of second jobs, though not so heavily concentrated in education. They found that 27 percent of the part-time faculty were teaching either in colleges or in elementary or secondary schools, 17 percent were employed in business, 13 percent were employed in government, and 12 percent were employed in industry (pp. 27–29).

Career aspirations and work histories are heavily influenced by motivations for teaching part time, of course. Leslie, Kellams, and Gunne (1982) gathered data through 104 personal interviews at 14 different institutions. They were therefore able to pursue the reasons and attitudes behind decisions to teach part time (pp. 41–46). Some of their findings parallel Tuckman's results.

The leading motive for teaching part time was found to be intrinsic, a matter of personal satisfaction. Part-time faculty were teaching to achieve personal enjoyment, fulfillment, and accomplishment, to make a contribution to human development, or to escape from a routine, less satisfying environment. Some were teaching for the prestige or status attached to college-level instruction. Those with intrinsic motivation said they were stimulated by the interesting mix of students and that the intellectual environment provided a rewarding change of pace. They said they were revitalized and that their views were broadened by involvement with academic colleagues. They believed they were good at teaching and felt they received positive feedback from students (Leslie, Kellams, and Gunne 1982, pp. 41–43; Yang and Zak 1981, pp. 25–26).

The next most frequent major motivation was professional. Part-timers in this category were primarily dedicated to their full-time, nonacademic profession. Like Tuckman's full-mooners, they held positions in business, industry, or government or were self-employed as attorneys, accountants, musicians, psychologists, or artists. They viewed the local college and their primary vocation as forming a partnership of mutual benefit. They brought current field practice to the classroom; in turn, they were kept up to date with theoretical developments in their professions. A few saw the possibility of identifying among their students promising candidates to enter their fields and even their particular firms. Part-time teaching for this group was a logical extension of the serious pursuit of their vocation or profession (Leslie, Kellams, and Gunne 1982, pp. 43–44).

The leading motive for teaching part time was found to be intrinsic, a matter of personal satisfaction.

The third major motivation was career aspiration. Careerists, like Tuckman's hopeful full-timers, were part-timers who wanted full-time work as college teachers but who had had to settle for less. Leslie, Kellams, and Gunne found little evidence that part-time positions led to full-time employment: Many career aspirations were destined to be unrealized. Some career-minded part-timers put together several jobs in various institutions to earn a full income. In so doing, they said in the interviews, they wasted an inordinate amount of time traveling from one location to another, and some became cynical and hostile. Among this group were people who had chosen not to complete the doctoral degree and those who had career motives that were frustrated by situational factors such as domestic obligations (like Tuckman's homeworkers) or geographical immobility. In some cases, spouses who followed their mates were relegated to part-time teaching because of a lack of full-time openings in their fields or informal antinepotism policies (Leslie, Kellams, and Gunne 1982, pp. 44–45).

The least frequent motivation was economic. Most faculty responded that while the extra money was helpful, they had more important reasons for teaching. This response was not surprising, as pay for part-time faculty is usually modest. Some part-timers, however, said that their earnings were a significant and needed supplement to their income. Housewives, students, those employed part time in several positions, the semiretired, and those seeking entry into full-time college- or university-level teaching were more likely to view remuneration from part-time teaching as important to them though not necessarily more important than other motivations (Leslie, Kellams, and Gunne 1982, pp. 45–46). Yang and Zak (1981), by contrast, found in their survey that financial need was next in importance to intrinsic motivation among part-timers (pp. 26–27).

Characteristics of Current Employment
Table 9 shows the reasons why part-timers thought they were hired and provides information about rank, workload, and level of satisfaction. Thirty-four percent of the part-timers responded that they were hired into "new" positions. Tuckman speculates that some were hired into posi-

TABLE 9
SELECTED CHARACTERISTICS OF PART-TIME FACULTY: CURRENT EMPLOYMENT

	Semi-retired	Student	Hopeful Full-timer	Full-mooner	Home-worker	Part-mooner	Part-unknowner	All Part-timers
Reason hired								
Percent in new position[a]	52.6	33.0	33.3	29.3	36.7	36.5	37.7	33.9
Percent in permanent position[a]	22.7	14.3	11.9	18.6	21.4	16.4	19.1	16.6
Percent hired to meet enrollment overload[a]	8.6	11.4	16.9	7.0	11.1	7.3	6.7	10.0
Percent in evening or continuing education division[a]	45.7	55.6	51.4	74.9	34.0	64.0	56.0	59.7
Type of institution								
Percent at two-year institution	44.9	50.9	51.3	58.7	42.5	50.8	52.8	52.6
Percent at four-year institution	38.3	35.2	39.7	29.3	35.0	36.5	30.6	34.0
Percent at university	16.8	13.9	9.0	12.1	22.5	12.7	16.6	13.4
Rank								
Percent with rank of full professor	15.9	0.1	0.2	1.4	0.4	1.8	3.2	1.5
Percent with rank of associate professor	4.7	1.1	1.3	2.8	2.9	3.9	6.3	2.8
Percent with rank of assistant professor	0.9	2.5	7.1	3.3	8.4	5.5	6.8	4.7
Percent with rank of other[b]	74.8	91.9	85.3	85.9	82.8	83.5	78.1	85.4
Percent unranked	3.7	4.3	6.1	6.6	5.5	5.3	5.6	5.6
Workload								
Average contact hours	5.5	5.6	6.5	3.7	6.5	4.3	4.5	5.0
Average courses taught	1.6	1.6	1.9	1.2	1.6	1.5	1.3	1.5
Average total hours	15.1	15.4	18.0	9.5	17.5	11.6	13.8	13.5
Satisfaction								
Average level of satisfaction[c]	31.5	29.7	25.2	31.9	30.8	30.8	31.1	29.9

[a]Those responding "don't know" are excluded from the computations.
[b]Includes instructors, lecturers, assistant instructors, adjuncts, visiting professors, and persons who answered "other."
[c]Based on a maximum possible score of 50.

Source: Tuckman 1978, p. 311.

tions previously filled by full-timers and that some were hired into newly created or restructured positions. Fifty-three percent of the semiretireds were in a new position for them, reflecting the increasing tendency for full-time tenured faculty to reduce their workload as they approach retirement (Tuckman 1978, p. 312) and the proliferation of options for retirement that allow faculty to continue teaching a reduced load with or without the benefits of tenure.

Only 17 percent of part-time faculty were hired into what they considered were permanent positions; most part-timers were hired for temporary positions. Sixty percent were hired for evening or continuing education courses, and 10 percent were hired to meet enrollment overloads. Three out of four full-mooners and two out of three part-mooners were teaching evening or continuing education classes. Leslie, Kellams, and Gunne (1982) found that 53 percent of the higher education institutions they surveyed used part-time faculty for evening and weekend instruction and that 40 percent used part-timers for noncredit and off-campus instruction (p. 21).

Part-time faculty employment can be categorized as "planned" (permanent) or "contingency" (temporary) (McCabe and Brezner 1978). Planned part-time faculty positions are those for which the institution has a predetermined need. They are filled semester after semester, and the appointments usually are decided well before registration. Individuals in planned part-time positions usually possess special skills not otherwise available and needed only part time. The contingency category includes part-time faculty who are available as needed to meet demand. Appointment is for one semester at a time. Contingency part-timers permit an institution to adjust to shifting enrollment while maintaining a stable, regular faculty, thus providing job security for full-time faculty (McCabe and Brezner 1978, pp. 62–69).

Over 90 percent of the part-time faculty in Tuckman's study were unranked or were designated as instructors, lecturers, assistant instructors, adjuncts, or visiting professors. Most part-time faculty with academic rank were semiretireds.

The semiretireds, students, full-mooners, part-mooners, and part-unknowners were employed less than half time, teaching an average of 1.5 courses. Hopeful full-timers taught an average of 1.9 courses involving 18 contact hours a week, homeworkers an average of 1.6 course and 17.5 contact hours. The fact that part-timers, by and large, are employed less than half time at any one institution avoids legal challenges for tenure and eliminates the requirement to provide certain types of benefits.

The full-mooners, semiretireds, part-unknowners, home-workers, and part-mooners indicated the greatest degree of satisfaction with part-time employment.[3] Generally, these part-timers were satisfied with their careers and felt they had achieved some kind of equilibrium between part-time work and other activities (Tuckman 1978, p. 313). The hopeful full-timers indicated the least satisfaction with their current part-time faculty employment (4.7 points lower than the average), indicating their dissatisfaction with their inability to find a full-time position (Tuckman 1978, p. 311).

The part-time faculty population is chimerical (Leslie 1984). As a group, they are simultaneously continuing and temporary, core and peripheral, employed at widely varying levels of full-time equivalency. These differences should be accommodated in faculty employment policies and practices. Both individuals and institutions will be better served when different policies and practices are developed for different classifications of part-time faculty.

[3]Career satisfaction was measured by a 10-question index that assigned a value of five to the most positive response and a value of one to the least positive. Thus, a maximum score of 50 was possible.

CONSTRAINTS ON INSTITUTIONAL POLICY AND PRACTICE

What institutions view as justifiable behavior by the employer because of financial exigency, traditional practice, and other circumstances is often seen as unfair by part-time faculty. Conflict exists between the rights of part-timers and the interests of full-time faculty (Head 1979, p. 2). This chapter describes four basic constraints on colleges and universities that affect the employment of part-time faculty: legal decisions, collective bargaining agreements, state funding formulas, and standards established by accrediting agencies (Leslie, Kellams, and Gunne 1982, pp. 47–72).

Legal Issues

The rights of part-time faculty are contested legally in four major areas: property rights, equal protection, statutory rights, and decisions regarding the placement of part-timers in collective bargaining units under the legal principle of community of interest.[4]

Property rights

Faculty can be divided into three basic classes: permanent (tenured), probationary (tenure-track), and temporary (those serving in non-tenure-accruing capacities). The classification of faculty at public colleges and universities depends upon state statute or administrative code. At private universities, it depends on institutional regulations or contractual agreements. Nearly all part-time faculty are classified as temporary. Some part-time temporary faculty, however, are strongly committed to their positions and depend upon them for their income. These part-timers seek more equitable pay, additional fringe benefits, better support services, and some degree of job security. Desiring job security, continuing part-time faculty have attempted to upgrade their status from temporary to probationary or permanent. In this sense, they are claiming a property right to the position (Head 1979, pp. 9–10), and in recent years, litigation has increased by part-time faculty attempting to establish as a legal principle the concept that they have a property right to their jobs. The underlying premise

---

[4]The reader is referred to Head 1979; Head and Kelley 1978; Head and Leslie 1979; Leslie, Kellams, and Gunne 1982; and Whelan 1980 for more thorough discussion of these issues.

is that continuous service, whether full or part time, may establish a legitimate expectation of reappointment (Head 1979; Whelan 1980).

Two Supreme Court cases set legal precedent regarding the property rights of part-time faculty. In *Perry* v. *Sinderman* [408 U.S. 593 (1972)], the Supreme Court established that a series of short-term contracts may, under certain conditions, establish a legitimate expectation of reemployment. Sinderman, a teacher in the Texas state college system for 10 years, was awarded de facto tenure because of his long service and because the junior college where he taught expressed the spirit of tenure in its policies even though it had no de jure tenure system (Head and Kelley 1978, p. 42). The Supreme Court held that proof of such property right did not entitle a teacher to reinstatement: It only obligated college officials to grant a hearing where he could be informed of the grounds for not retaining him and challenge them. The Court noted, in explaining the concept of an implied contract, "A teacher . . . who has held his position for a number of years might be able to show from the circumstances of this service—and from other relevant facts—that he has a legitimate claim of entitlement to job tenure" (Leslie and Head 1979, p. 56).

Board of Regents v. *Roth* [408 U.S. 564 (1972)] is a complementary case. The Supreme Court warned:

> *To have a property interest in a benefit, a person clearly must have more than an abstract need or desire for it. He must have more than a unilateral expectation of it. He must, instead, have a legitimate claim of entitlement to it* (Head 1979, p. 11).

A legitimate claim is established not by the Constitution but by existing rules or understandings that stem from an independent source, such as state law. Part-time faculty must show that not renewing their contract resulted from violation of a constitutional right or must demonstrate a property right by statute, by contract, or by general institutional understanding. Otherwise, they are not entitled to procedural due process. For these reasons, state statutes often control in matters relating to the status of part-time faculty in public institutions (Head 1979, p. 11). In private institutions, it is not likely that any constitutional right to continued employment exists. The only way a constitutional right might be established would be through proof that a nominally private institution had become an instrumentality of the state (Whelan 1980, p. 20).

Part-time faculty are normally hired on short-term contracts that contain nonrenewal clauses. How do such circumstances allow part-time faculty to establish legitimate claims to continuous employment? Key considerations may be length of service and institutional practices. In *Balen* v. *the Peralta Junior College District* (1974), the California Supreme Court recognized both factors by ruling in favor of a part-time instructor who argued that his length of service gave him statutory property rights to classification as a probationary employee. Balen was a part-time faculty member continuously rehired to teach the same class, semester after semester, for 4½ years. Administrators notified him verbally in the fall of 1969 that he would not be reemployed in the spring, which coincided with his attempt to organize other part-time faculty members, purportedly to protect their interests. The California Supreme Court held that Balen was properly classified in a status entitling him by statute to "pretermination notice and hearing." The case was nationally significant because it relied on the ruling from the U.S. Supreme Court in *Perry* v. *Sinderman* to reach its major conclusion that "the essence of the statutory classification system is that continuity of service restricts the power to terminate employment which the institution's governing body would normally possess" (Fryer 1977, pp. 16–17). Common institutional practice, in addition to continuous service, can establish reasonable expectation of reemployment. The Peralta Junior College District, Balen's employer, routinely terminated all part-time faculty each year. It just as routinely rehired them, in what might be described as an administrative strategy designed to meet the letter of the law. In reviewing this practice, the California Supreme Court noted:

Such an administrative practice of routine blanket dismissals to circumvent proper classification carries with it concomitant liability; i.e., the form letter dismissal with virtually automatic rehiring creates an expectancy of reemployment (Leslie and Head 1979, p. 57).

The decision in *Balen* laid the foundation for *Peralta Federation of Teachers, Local 1603 AFT* v. *Peralta Community College District,* which was heard in the Alameda County Superior Court in 1975. This case made it possible for part-time faculty to receive tenure in two or more school districts at the same time. Consistent with statutory changes in 1967, the county court ordered that tenure be granted to seven employees who had been employed before 1967 (when the statute was amended to allow community colleges to hire temporary faculty indefinitely) on a part-time basis for three consecutive years. Probationary status was granted to five others who had been employed before 1967 and had entered their second consecutive year of employment when they were dismissed. Seventeen other individuals not named in the case who provided supporting documents that they were part-time employees at Peralta before 1967 and in addition were still part-time employees of the district in 1979 also were granted tenure (Fryer 1977, pp. 17–18).*

The California legislature has blocked further rulings similar to *Balen* and *Peralta Federation of Teachers* with a statute that explicitly limits the application of continuous employment to faculty who teach more than 60 percent of a normal full-time teaching load:

> *Notwithstanding any other provision to the contrary, any person who is employed to teach adult or community college classes for not more than 60 percent of the hours per week considered a full-time assignment for regular employees having comparable duties, shall be classified as a temporary employee, and shall not become a contract employee . . .* (California Education Code, §87482, operative April 30, 1977).

Connecticut also has addressed the issue of workload. The state Board of Labor Relations divided faculty members protected under that state's collective bargaining statute into groups working more than and fewer than 7½ contact hours per week. Part-timers carrying more than 7½

*Peralta Community College Board of Trustees 1984, unpublished information.

hours per week enjoy protection—most significantly, inclusion in the bargaining unit—while those carrying lighter workloads do not.

The significance of workload as a factor in securing property rights is emphasized by the fact that about two-thirds of all colleges and universities nationwide restrict the amount of work a part-time faculty member can perform (Leslie and Head 1979, pp. 58–59).

Clearly, part-time faculty in some jurisdictions can establish a property right to continued employment or at least can establish a right to procedural protection before employment is terminated. It is equally clear, however, that they cannot establish such rights in all jurisdictions. Local conditions, including common practice on individual campuses, statutory provisions, and explicit contractual terms all affect the rights of part-time faculty to continued employment (Head and Kelley 1978, p. 43). The cases cited above notwithstanding, part-time faculty normally enjoy only evanescent contractual ties with the employing institution. They teach for one term at a time, with a contract that promises nothing else. The offer of renewal is at the discretion of the employing institutions. And when institutions are careful about their policies and practices and comply with statutory provisions, it is difficult for part-timers to establish property rights in court (Leslie, Kellams, and Gunne 1982, p. 48).

Equal protection
Suits that allege denial of equal protection of the law to part-time faculty focus on equal pay and benefits. These cases are usually unsuccessful, and three grounds of refutation are common.

First, institutions can argue that part-time faculty are usually assigned fewer tasks than full-time faculty. Even if they teach a prorated number of courses, they have fewer duties relating to research, administration, advising students, and public service. Therefore, the argument goes, they cannot claim to be performing equal work on the basis of teaching alone. Second, most part-time faculty have more limited preparation, both academic and pedagogical, and less teaching experience than do full-time faculty. Accordingly, they would be paid at the lower end of the scale if they were hired as full-time faculty (Leslie, Kellams, and

Gunne 1982, pp. 52–53). Some observers dispute this claim, however. Tuckman's research indicates that at least some part-time faculty are as well prepared as, if not better than, their full-time counterparts (Tuckman 1978; Tuckman and Vogler 1979). Third, if all part-time faculty received prorated pay and benefits, institutions would have little economic incentive to hire part-time faculty. Colleges and universities can argue that they use part-timers because they cannot support enough full-time positions.

If part-timers were to work at the same rate of pay as full-timers, a serious deficit in the college budget would result. It would cost Los Angeles Community College District an additional ten million dollars a year to pay part-timers this way (Koltai 1977, p. 18).

In arguing for equal protection, part-time faculty must show that a classification distinguishing between part-time and full-time employment for purposes of establishing pay is arbitrary and unreasonable. If part- and full-time faculty are essentially alike in qualifications, characteristics, abilities, functions, duties, and activities, then paying part-timers proportionately less than full-timers may constitute an unreasonable and arbitrary employment practice. In *Peralta Federation of Teachers,* a leading case in this respect, the union argued that equal pay for equal work is required by the Fourteenth Amendment and that part- and full-time teachers are essentially equal in credentials, functions, and duties. The defendant district denied that its policy conflicted with the equal protection clause of the Fourteenth Amendment, arguing that part-timers had less experience, limited credentials, and fewer functions to perform. The district also argued that its poor financial status prevented paying part-timers equally. The county court upheld the district's policy of paying temporary faculty less than prorated pay, but the union appealed and the appellate court determined that the employees who had been awarded regular status by the county court were also granted prorated wages as back pay. Employees who had been denied regular or contract status were also denied prorated pay. The appellate court upheld the argument of poor financial status as a reason for paying temporary or noncontract part-time faculty less than full-time faculty

Part-time faculty normally . . . teach for one term at a time, with a contract that promises nothing else.

(Head 1979, p. 28; Head and Kelley 1978, p. 48; Whelan 1980, p. 21).

Different qualifications and assignments among part-time faculty complicate questions of compensation. The most difficult problem for some institutions is not how to prorate the pay and benefits of part-time faculty against those of full-time faculty but how to establish equitable compensation plans for part-time faculty who differ widely among themselves. Case law concerning equal protection and equal pay has tended to sustain the institutions' case against prorating pay for part-time faculty, but colleges and universities with formal classification systems and pay scales for part-time faculty that recognize the differences among this highly diverse group of individuals are in a better legal position than those that do not (Leslie, Kellams, and Gunne 1982, p. 54).[5]

Statutory rights

Much litigation about the rights of part-time faculty centers on statutory provisions, and the variation from state to state is so great that generalizations about statutory protection are not possible. This section therefore discusses one example of protection from state statutes.

Statutory protection of the rights of part-time faculty has been most thoroughly debated in California (Leslie and Head 1979). California statutes have long classified public school teachers as permanent or probationary. In 1967, the code governing public school teachers was amended to treat the special case of community colleges. Institutions were given the right to hire temporary faculty for indefinite periods without any obligation to grant them probationary status. After *Balen*, the statutory provisions were amended to limit the opportunity to become probationary faculty to those who taught more than 60 percent of the hours per week considered full-time. After the statute was amended, part-time faculty could assume loads greater than 60 percent of a full-time load if they did not work at this level for more than two semesters or quarters during any three con-

[5]The legal precedents discussed under "equal protection" may soon be obsolete. Although recent legislation and court cases about "comparable worth" have addressed the compensation of workers outside academe, the concept of comparable worth could have a considerable impact on the salaries of part-time faculty in the near future.

secutive academic years. Thus, California has grappled with the issue of part-timers' rights to employment security through variables such as workload and continuous service. The courts' inability to consistently resolve the issue is indeed a "bowl of spaghetti," however (Koltai 1977).

Head (1979) surveyed a sample of community colleges in California to determine the impact of legal decisions on hiring part-time faculty. The responding colleges indicated that legal decisions did affect their policies. The major influence reported was greater control over the use of part-time faculty. Essentially, California community colleges control part-time faculty in two ways: (1) by reducing the teaching load to a percentage that by statute does not allow achievement of probationary or permanent status, and (2) by replacing part-time faculty as much as possible with full-time faculty. Two colleges in the survey said they had restricted all part-time instruction to 40 percent or less of a full-time load. All institutions reported that court decisions had caused changes in scheduling that limited the previous use of part-time faculty in some areas. In effect, court decisions have led some California community colleges to deny increased employment to part-time faculty who sought from the courts greater property rights, equal protection under the law, and job security (Head 1979, p. 50).

The regulation of employment (which includes postsecondary education) was greatly accelerated during the 1970s, marked by expanded efforts in enforcement on the part of the executive and judicial branches. Federal laws and regulations, including Title VII of the Civil Rights Act, Executive Order 11246 as amended (affirmative action), the Age Discrimination in Employment Act, the Rehabilitation Act, the Equal Pay Act, and the Fair Labor Standards Act, indirectly provide statutory protection for part-time faculty. Equal employment opportunity, occupational safety and health, and equity in employment practices are some of the concepts that have generated more than a dozen legislative acts in the past two decades (National Association 1983).

Collective Bargaining
Overview
The 1970s saw an enormous increase in collective bargaining in American higher education. In 1981, there were

more than 680 unionized campuses. Nationally, more than one in four faculty and professional staff had joined a union. Not all segments of higher education were equally represented in this explosion of interest in unions, however. Of 681 unionized institutions, 428 (63 percent) were two-year colleges, but fewer than 100 private colleges and universities were unionized. Few public and private institutions commonly regarded as prestigious have faculty unions. Although far more two-year institutions are unionized, four-year institutions, because of their size, account for two-thirds of all unionized faculty members. In the present decade, unionization of faculty in public colleges and universities has been slowed by the absence of collective bargaining laws in half the states (Baldridge, Kemerer, and Associates 1981, p. 1).

Part-time faculty present a dilemma for unions. The use of part-time faculty appears to be a management tool to reduce costs, which results in the displacement of union members. If the number of part-time faculty continues to increase and if state employee relations boards continue to follow California's lead in including part-time faculty in the bargaining unit, faculty unions may well respond more directly to part-timers' needs. The percentage of contracts containing provisions pertaining to part-time faculty increased from 21 percent in 1973 to 36 percent in 1979, in community colleges from 21 percent to 58 percent (Baldridge, Kemerer, and Associates 1981, p. 26). Given the heavy use of part-time faculty by community colleges, the greatest opportunity for gains in collective bargaining for part-timers is probably in that sector. On some campuses, they may become the primary beneficiaries of collective bargaining. In the Los Angeles community college system, for example, the union has attempted to secure tenure for part-time faculty. While unsuccessful, union leaders say they will try again (Baldridge, Kemerer, and Associates 1981, p. 27).

Part-timers' inclusion in the bargaining unit
The right of part-timers to bargain with employers varies in higher education. Private institutions are covered by the National Labor Relations Act, which does not speak directly to part-time professional employees. Consequently, the National Labor Relations Board (NLRB) decides

whether part-time faculty will be included in the bargaining unit after reviewing the facts on a case-by-case basis. At public institutions, the right to bargain is established by state statute. Roughly half the states provide for faculty bargaining, and the rights of part-time faculty vary from state to state.

In deciding the first cases involving such determination for part-time faculty, the NLRB relied on earlier decisions relating to part-time employment in industry. In industry, part-time employees are regarded as regular employees and included in the bargaining unit, or they are regarded as casual or irregular employees and are excluded. The brief prepared by management for *The University of Connecticut* v. *the University of Connecticut Chapter of the AAUP* describes the difficulty of translating industrial precedent into workable solutions for higher education:

> . . . *The case demonstrates the degree to which those of us who represent higher education management during this period of intense collective bargaining activity are likely to find ourselves held captive by earlier labor board decisions. All of which, whether they be in the area of unit determination, or, as in the present case, workload, were fashioned with environments other than universities in mind. Those of us who represent our trustees at the bargaining table or before labor boards must deal not only with the problem of how to transplant the industrial organ called collective bargaining into the body of higher education without killing the recipient. We must also distinguish our particular institution from others and from labor board decisions predicated on someone else's workplace* (Geetter 1981, p. 254).

The NLRB decided the first cases involving faculty in 1971. In two cases at Long Island University, the two candidates for the bargaining agent, the American Federation of Teachers (AFT) and the AAUP, wanted a bargaining unit consisting of all faculty, while the university's governing board wanted to exclude part-time faculty. The NLRB ruled for inclusion of part-timers, stating that it could find no clear pattern or practice of collective bargaining in academe that would cause it to modify existing guidelines for determining bargaining units in industry. The precedent of including part-time faculty was followed at Fordham University and at the University of New Haven (Head and Leslie 1979, pp. 363–64).

Some institutions in which part-timers gained bargaining rights expressed great dissatisfaction, pointing out that the initial NLRB decisions ignored the needs of full-time faculty and that the large percentage of part-time faculty in those institutions posed a threat to full-time faculty. At the Brooklyn Center of Long Island University, for example, 19 percent of the faculty were part-time, at C. W. Post Center of Long Island University 38 percent, at Fordham 33 percent, and at the University of New Haven 67 percent. The NLRB was petitioned to review its position (Head and Leslie 1979, p. 365) and totally reversed its position in a landmark case involving New York University in 1973. The prime determinant for the composition of a bargaining unit, according to the NLRB, was a community or mutuality of interest in wages, hours, and working conditions. To assess this community of interest, the NLRB used four major criteria: compensation, participation in university governance, eligibility for tenure, and working conditions. The greater the community of interest between part-time and full-time faculty, based upon these criteria, the greater the chances of their inclusion in a single bargaining unit (Head and Leslie 1979; Whelan 1980). In its decision, the NLRB concluded:

After careful reflection, we have reached the conclusion that part-time faculty do not share a community of interest with full-time faculty and, therefore, should not be included in the same bargaining unit (Head and Leslie 1979, p. 365).

Most cases brought to the NLRB since the New York University decision have resulted in the exclusion of part-timers.

Considerable inconsistency has marked the decisions of state labor relations boards regarding part-time faculty and the inclusion of part-timers in bargaining units at public institutions. This inconsistency is exemplified in the decisions of the New York Public Employee Relations Board (PERB) with respect to the City University of New York (CUNY) and the State University of New York (SUNY) in the late 1960s. At SUNY, PERB approved a single unit for the university's entire professional staff. Sixteen thousand professional employees were involved, and even though none of the parties had requested it, 2,000 part-time faculty were included. In contrast, part-time faculty were excluded from the bargaining unit at CUNY because, according to PERB, they were nearly as numerous as full-time faculty and their primary commitments were off campus. Three years later, when the collective bargaining contracts at CUNY were expiring, the parties reversed their earlier positions. Union officials demanded one unit for all instructional personnel, while the university wanted separate units for full-time faculty, part-time faculty, and non-teaching personnel. PERB resolved the proposed reversal by allowing employees to vote on whether they desired a single unit. The vote favored the single unit (Head and Leslie 1979, p. 369).

Although rulings have been inconsistent across states, public labor relations boards are more prone to include part-time faculty within the full-time bargaining unit than is the NLRB. In making their decisions, they use the same criteria the NLRB used in the New York University case to deny participation to part-time faculty. An example is the University of Massachusetts decision (1976). Union officials supported a faculty collective bargaining unit that would include part-time faculty; the governing board opposed it. The Massachusetts Labor Relations Commission deliberated for two years (the longest deliberation in its history) before determining that part-timers who had taught at least one course for three consecutive semesters were eligible for inclusion in the bargaining unit for full-time faculty. The commission found that part-timers generally performed the same qualitative duties that full-timers performed and received many of the same fringe benefits. Although they were not authorized to sit on the Faculty Senate, part-time faculty participated in departmental and collegiate governance. Furthermore, evaluation procedures were substantially the same for part- and full-time faculty. The only significant difference between the two groups was eligibility for tenure, which the commission stated was not a true indication of community of interest (Head and Kelley 1978; Head and Leslie 1979; Leslie, Kellams, and Gunne 1982).

A similar decision was made in California for Los Rios Community College in 1977. The California Teachers Association, National Education Association, and Los Rios College Federation of Teachers urged that part-time faculty be included with full-time faculty in a single bargaining unit, while the community college district urged their exclusion. The state board ruled that all part-time instructors who taught classes for an equivalent of three of the preceding six semesters should be included, basing the decision on the same criteria used to include part-timers in the University of Massachusetts decision and exclude part-timers in the New York University decision (Head and Kelley 1978, p. 54; Head and Leslie 1979, pp. 373–75).

The trend toward including part-time faculty established in the California community colleges was continued in the recently ratified agreement between the Board of Trustees of the California State University and the California Faculty Association (California State University 1983). In the recognition clause, the parties agreed to exclude from the bargaining unit only faculty employed for 60 or fewer days, summer session faculty employed in a particular classification, or department chairs if they were appointed for 12 months and were assigned at least 60 percent administrative duties (p. 2). This sweeping recognition clause effectively includes all faculty, from graduate students to partial-year (nine-month) department chairs.

National studies of collective bargaining quantify the variation among contracts regarding the inclusion of part-time faculty in the bargaining unit. The National Center for the Study of Collective Bargaining in Higher Education (NCSCBHE) reviewed 139 contracts at two-year colleges in 1976. It found that half the contracts studied did not consider part-time faculty as members of the bargaining unit. The exclusion was achieved explicitly or by definition of the coverage. Recognition clauses specifically stated that part-time or adjunct faculty were excluded or that the faculty association was the exclusive bargaining representative for all full-time faculty. About 43 percent of the contracts included part-time faculty in one of three ways: (1) by specifying that all part-time faculty were included, (2) by referring to all faculty, or (3) by making inclusion in the bargaining unit contingent upon workload. The privilege of being in the bargaining unit could be accompanied by the responsibility to pay union dues or representation fees (NCSCBHE 1977).

Of 89 collective bargaining agreements in effect at four-year institutions as of the end of December 1979, 45 percent stated that only full-time faculty were eligible to be in the bargaining unit, while 33 percent explicitly included part-time faculty. Most of the agreements limited how little part-timers could teach and still be members of the bargaining unit. The remaining contracts simply spoke of faculty without distinguishing between full-time and part-time status (Johnstone 1981, pp. 137–38).

Before deciding whether or not part-time faculty should be included in campus bargaining units, labor boards customarily examine the terms of employment, working conditions, and characteristics of part-time faculty within a particular institution or system. The Connecticut State Board of Labor Relations ruling in *The University of Connecticut* v. *the University of Connecticut Chapter of the AAUP* (1977) is an example of careful scrutiny of the workload of part-time faculty. The board had determined earlier that a member of the technical college faculty who taught half the average contact hours of full-time faculty at his or her institution would be eligible for inclusion in the bargaining unit. During hearings, management argued for a refinement of this ruling, maintaining that workload differs:

> *Few would argue that humanists work less hard than scientists, or that preparation of a 3-hour philosophy course is necessarily less rigorous than preparing a science course earning the same credits but distributed over more contact hours. . . . If the University were required to adopt the Technical College standard, special payroll lecturers who taught two English courses, i.e., six . . . contact hours would be out of the unit while those who taught two chemistry courses (eight . . . contact hours) would be included* (Geetter 1981, pp. 261–62).

In addition, management argued that using contact hours as a criterion makes no allowance for differences in difficulty between teaching undergraduate or advanced doctoral courses. It argued also that contact hours do not measure the difference in workload between teaching one course twice and teaching two courses requiring separate preparations. Finally, management maintained that teachers' contact hours vary from term to term and from year to year, depending upon career patterns. The board agreed with management and stipulated that the computation for eligibility in a bargaining unit could not include laboratory supervision or teaching the same course twice (Geetter 1981, pp. 260–61).

Whether or not they can be included in the campus bargaining unit is crucial to part-time faculty because it offers a direct vehicle for securing better working conditions. Once a community of interest has been established between part-time and full-time faculty, a rationale is available for claims by part-time faculty concerning status and compensation. If working conditions are virtually identical for part- and full-time faculty, it can be argued that both groups share an interest in property. Then part-time faculty can claim rights to permanent status or tenure and to identical or prorated pay schedules. Various state labor boards have inconsistently applied the principle of community of interest. The trend is to continue using the criteria established by the NLRB in the New York University decision but to apply them with differing results. More important than past bargaining history, type of institution, or geographical location are the differences among part-time faculty themselves, particularly their function and workload (Head and Leslie 1979, pp. 376–78).

Other contract provisions
Collective bargaining contracts are frequently vehicles for protecting the interests of full-timers. Unions have not yet proved that they can serve as effective representatives of both full-timers' and part-timers' interests, and the dichotomy of interests between the two groups appears to thwart a stable accommodation (Leslie and Ikenberry 1979, pp. 21–25). Some part-time faculty have sought to avoid dependence on groups representing full-time faculty by organizing separately and negotiating for themselves. For example, part-timers originally formed a separate unit at CUNY but subsequently merged with full-time faculty into a single unit. Although a separate unit for part-timers ex-

ists at Portland State University in Oregon, the agreement focuses on procedures and provides few direct rights or benefits for the part-timers it covers (Leslie 1984, p. 14).

Unless temporary and part-time faculty are members of the bargaining unit or unless their appointment, salary, and working conditions affect working conditions of full-time faculty, it is illegal for the union and employer to bargain their conditions of employment. If part-time faculty are part of the unit, however, or if their employment affects full-timers' working conditions, then the contract can be written to protect the rights of full-time faculty. By and large, this is what has happened.

The contract usually defines the nature of the appointment and its source, including the assignment of workload and the institution's responsibility or lack thereof for covering full-time faculty positions (Goodwin 1977). A pervasive theme in contracts is the protection of the full-time faculty's workload. Full-time faculty usually have priority for preferred teaching assignments and can bump part-time faculty from their positions (Leslie and Ikenberry 1979). In some institutions, the hiring of part-time faculty is restricted, either departmentwide or collegewide. The Oakland (California) Community College contract specifies, for example, that the number of part-time faculty on the campus shall not exceed 35 percent of the full-time faculty (NCSCBHE 1977).

Collective bargaining contracts generally do not grant part-time faculty meaningful roles in making decisions about such matters as choosing department chairs, determining membership on faculty evaluation or curriculum committees, and making departmental assignments (Goodwin 1977).

Part-time faculty are rarely eligible for tenure. Most collective bargaining agreements categorically deny eligibility for tenure to part-time faculty or state that eligibility for tenure will be at the discretion of the institution's chief executive (Goodwin 1977). A survey by the College and University Personnel Association showed that 87 percent of the responding institutions did not award tenure to part-time faculty. While unionized institutions are slightly more likely to award tenure to part-time continuing faculty (Baldridge, Kemerer, and Associates 1981, pp. 26–27),

Collective bargaining contracts are frequently vehicles for protecting the interests of full-timers.

---

virtually no institutions give temporary part-timers any rights of tenure.

Clauses covering retrenchment are written to the detriment of the part-time faculty's interests (Goodwin 1977; Leslie and Ikenberry 1979; Lozier 1977; NCSCBHE 1977). They generally do not support affirmative action goals and gains, because affirmative action hires are not usually given special consideration (Baldridge, Kemerer, and Associates 1981, p. 30; Lozier 1977, p. 245). In times of retrenchment, part-time temporary faculty are cut first, followed in order by full-time temporary faculty, probationary faculty, and tenured faculty. Of 258 contracts studied, 40 percent stated that part-time temporary faculty would be cut first, and 22 percent provided some form of protection for part-time faculty through seniority rights or by restricting retrenchment to specific departments or fields (Leslie and Ikenberry 1979, p. 22). If a full-time position can no longer be sustained, part-time positions may be eliminated to maintain a full-time faculty member, if that person is qualified for the altered assignment. And a retrenched full-time faculty member has the first option on available part-time assignments.

Part-time faculty have fared well in collective bargaining with respect to compensation. In Leslie and Ikenberry's study (1979), 33 percent of the sample contracts provided prorated pay; in a broader sample of both union and non-union institutions, only 21 percent reported prorated pay. In 56 percent of the contracts, some part-time faculty were made eligible for at least some fringe benefits (p. 23).

Part-time faculty have occasional access to grievance procedures. But only a few contracts allow the pursuit of a grievance to arbitration (Leslie and Ikenberry 1979, p. 23). In the California State University contract, part-time temporary faculty have access to grievance procedures for alleged violations of the terms of the contract and for alleged punitive reassignment during the period of appointment (California State University 1983).

These contract provisions indicate that part-time faculty generally do not benefit greatly from being included in the bargaining unit with full-time faculty. To date, too few part-time faculty have been union members and they have been too diverse in their needs to exert a real influence on contract negotiations.

The unions' positions on part-timers

The three national faculty unions—AAUP, NEA, and AFT—hold slightly different positions regarding representation of the interests of part-time faculty.

AAUP has a long history of developing policy statements governing faculty employment practices for use by institutions (Furniss 1978). In 1975, AAUP began to systematically consider the status of part-time faculty. Recognizing the economic and political threat posed by part-time faculty—seeing part-timers as independent contractors who could undercut the market and skirt the performance reviews and tenure decisions required for full-time faculty—AAUP also realized that part-time work was the only route to an academic career for those whose aspirations were thwarted by tight markets and family obligations. Based in part on Tuckman's research, the Committee W report at the annual meeting in 1977 recommended that part-timers be eligible for tenure and for salary and benefits on a prorated basis and that part-timers be subjected to the association's up-or-out rule (Gray 1977). In 1981, the AAUP's Committee A on Academic Freedom and Tenure published an extensive statement on the status of part-time faculty that recommended tenure rights for part-time faculty, longer periods for notice that an appointment was not being renewed, and access to due process and grievance procedures. It also advocated prorated salaries and benefits for part-time faculty who perform a full range of faculty functions (Stern et al. 1981). AAUP has yet to resolve these conflicting realities, however, and to take a final position on the rights of part-timers (Leslie, Kellams, and Gunne 1982, p. 60).

In 1976, the National Education Association labeled the the use or abuse of part-time faculty a major problem in higher education, noting that part-time faculty can be used to exclude career professionals. The ability of part-time faculty to work outside the framework of collective bargaining and professional certification, it said, makes them a "core of unregulated personnel" that can be exploited by unscrupulous administrators and boards of trustees. The NEA argues that nonunion labor will work for lower wages, thus undercutting gains made by union members. Its aim is to raise part-time wages to prorated FTE rates and to encourage employment of a single full-time instructor whenever part-time assignments can feasibly be combined (Leslie 1978a, p. 4).

In 1977, AFT passed a resolution opposing increased reliance on part-time faculty. AFT's position is similar to NEA's: Part-time faculty undercut the financial security and the laboriously won rights to seniority, peer review, and due process of full-time faculty. The AFT contends that the use of part-time faculty to undermine the salaries and standards of full-time faculty also exploits part-time faculty (Leslie, Kellams, and Gunne 1982; McCabe and Brezner 1978).

Essentially, the three national faculty unions want to minimize and control the use of part-time faculty. They argue for fewer part-time faculty members and greater economic and professional security for those few. A sufficiently large and mobilized part-time contingent in the union might cause an internal split. Part-time faculty, for example, might be ambivalent about tenure but feel strongly about economic issues, while full-time faculty might want to emphasize job security rather than high salaries in a declining market. The result could be a less than united front at the bargaining table (Leslie, Kellams, and Gunne 1982, pp. 61–63).

Other Constraints

For public institutions, a significant constraint on institutional policy and practices regarding the use of part-time faculty is state-imposed funding formulas. Funding formulas can constrain the use of part-timers in a variety of ways. Some states regulate the ratio of part- to full-time faculty without allowing conversion of positions. In one case, full-time ranks serve as a base for the budget request, essentially ignoring part-time faculty. The ratio of full-time faculty to students can be the funding base so that an increase in students is followed by an increase in full-time faculty (Leslie, Kellams, and Gunne 1982, p. 67). Not only can state boards of higher education or legislatures restrict the use of part-time faculty; state systems can also employ similar formulas. In the California State University system, part-time faculty positions are budgeted at one salary level, while full-time faculty positions are budgeted at the rank and salary step the incumbent holds (California State University and Colleges 1977). The need to balance sala-

ries of part-time faculty at the budgeted salary level limits
the number of part-time faculty that can be employed and
the salary they can be paid, particularly in fields like business and computer science, where it is difficult to find qualified individuals.

The fourth and final constraint on institutional use of
part-time faculty is standards set by accrediting agencies.
The increased use of part-time faculty has become a concern of both regional and professional accrediting agencies.
Visiting accrediting teams scrutinize personnel rosters for
part-time faculty and ask for verification of their experience and credentials; they examine orientation programs
and communication processes between full- and part-time
faculty (Ernst and McFarlane 1978).

No language or format is commonly used among accrediting agencies for reporting about part-time faculty, but of
accrediting agencies that responded to one survey, none
regulate the use of part-time faculty in any specific way.
Standards the accrediting agencies use affect part-time
faculty employment, however (Leslie, Kellams, and Gunne
1982). Some standards set quantitative limits on the use of
part-time faculty. The American Assembly of Collegiate
Schools of Business, for example, requires 75 percent of
the FTE staff to be employed on a full-time basis.

Accrediting agencies also can control quality by limiting
teaching loads and student/faculty ratios. They can expect
faculty to have certain credentials and to exercise control
over academic policy. Part-time faculty do not necessarily
hold these credentials and are not usually in a position to
participate in academic policy making. Other standards
could be interpreted as discouraging the use of part-timers:
continuous and active involvement in their profession,
continuing professional development, creative activity, and
research. By contrast, professional programs requiring
accreditation approve the use of practitioners in the field as
part-time faculty. The American Bar Association, the Association of Theological Schools, and the American Soci-
ety of Foresters have advocated the employment of part-
time faculty with a wide range of experience in the field.

Thus, such standards appear to support the limited and
educationally justifiable use of part-time faculty for particular purposes, while favoring the preservation of academic
quality that only a full-time core faculty can provide. At

least two institutions, however, have achieved regional accreditation with virtually all instruction provided by part-time faculty (Leslie, Kellams, and Gunne 1982, p. 71).

Summing It Up

The two basic realities of part-time faculty employment— that part-timers vary widely in their qualifications, needs, and career aspirations and that institutions also vary in the numbers and ways in which they use part-timers—have led to confusion and inconsistency in court and labor board rulings. In this legal environment, the best protection for colleges and universities is to clearly specify the conditions of employment for part-timers. Institutions of higher education need carefully developed contracts for the appointment of part-time faculty that specify the institution's requirements and the part-timers' rights. While part-time faculty possess few rights of property or equal protection, they should be given the basic human right of thoughtful, deliberate, and fair consideration of their interests in equitable compensation and job security. Where colleges and universities have had legal problems, they have generally been the result of the failure to provide or to follow carefully developed and widely disseminated, written policies and practices that govern all aspects of part-time faculty employment and take into account the diversity among part-timers.

Whether or not part-time faculty should be included in the faculty collective bargaining unit has been an issue since academic collective bargaining began. Even when part-time faculty are part of the unit and covered by the collective bargaining contract, their treatment is usually less than equal and full-time faculty are usually the primary beneficiaries of the contract. The determination of whether to include part-timers in the bargaining unit and the negotiation of contracts should be conducted with an understanding of the situation on each campus. The results of negotiation should be protection of the critical areas of concern expressed by many part-time faculty and a concomitant recognition of their positive role in the institution's academic life (Leslie and Ikenberry 1979, pp. 25–26).

INSTITUTIONAL POLICIES AND PRACTICES

College and university policies and practices regarding the employment of part-time faculty are shaped by many influences—by institutional needs, missions, and traditions; by the diverse characteristics of part-time faculty; by the academic labor market; and by legal constraints. These policies and practices affect the recruitment and hiring of part-timers, their assignments and workload, support services, communication with peers and participation in governance, compensation and fringe benefits, and job security.

Recruitment and Hiring

Responsibility for hiring part-time faculty is usually delegated to academic departments. In a statewide survey of California community colleges, 41 percent reported that departments had full responsibility for screening and recommending the appointment of part-time faculty (Sewell, Brydon, and Plosser 1976). While authority to hire is normally given to departments, however, monitoring part-time employment and allocating faculty positions is usually retained by the central administration (Leslie, Kellams, and Gunne 1982, p. 76).

Some colleges and universities use full-scale search and selection procedures in response to affirmative action regulations that affect the hiring of part-time faculty. Others feel that part-time faculty are exempt from requirements for affirmative action. Seventy-six percent of respondent California community colleges in one survey, for example, reported that the affirmative action policy was applied in the same way in hiring both part-time and full-time faculty (Sewell, Brydon, and Plosser 1976).

Part-timers are usually recruited from the local labor market. In one study, 72 percent of the institutions reported that they hired part-time faculty from the immediate area, an additional 15 percent hired from within a 30-mile radius of the campus, and just under 10 percent hired part-time faculty from the region (Leslie, Kellams, and Gunne 1982). Virtually no institutions hired part-time faculty on a national basis (Leslie, Kellams, and Gunne 1982; Parsons 1980a). This emphasis on local recruiting is consistent with Tuckman's findings. Except for students and hopeful full-timers, fewer than 40 percent of the part-time faculty in his study were free to move (Tuckman 1978, pp. 311–13). Because recruiting is essentially local, the quality and diversity of the pool from which part-time faculty are drawn vary greatly from one institution to the next.

Trying to recruit and hire part-time faculty solely from a local market has certain competitive disadvantages: (1) The shortages of personnel may be acute in highly specialized fields; (2) part-time teaching schedules may discourage well-qualified people from applying; (3) institutions may find that their salary scales put them at a disadvantage in a crowded market; and (4) the lack of transportation and sufficient work or more continuous work may discourage well-qualified individuals. Nonetheless, part-time faculty continue to be recruited mainly from the local market because almost no one will relocate for part-time work (Leslie, Kellams, and Gunne 1982, p. 75).

The search may entail formal, written procedures. Hagerstown Junior College in Maryland, for example, recruits extensively in the local secondary school system and in business and industry, occasionally using newspaper advertisements. Full-time faculty are encouraged to recommend candidates. The search committee, in collaboration with the appropriate division head, screens applicants and recommends its choices to the dean of instruction (Parsons 1980b, pp. 48–49).

More institutions, however (more than 60 percent of the reporting institutions in the study by Leslie, Kellams, and Gunne), find their most effective recruitment is informal personal contact with potential candidates. Some do not recruit actively. Acquaintances and community contacts are the main sources for applicants. Part-time faculty themselves or individuals interested in becoming part-timers actively seek the work (Grymes 1976, pp. 25–28; Leslie, Kellams, and Gunne 1982, p. 73).

Over half of the institutions in Leslie, Kellams, and Gunne's survey hire part-time faculty according to enrollment, and most appointments are for one term at a time. Only 18 percent of the institutions reported once-a-year hiring cycles. When hiring part-time faculty is based on enrollment, the administration ensures that enrollment is sufficient to guarantee all full-time faculty full teaching loads before making any commitment to part-time faculty. Occasionally part-time faculty are carried at lower salaries when enrollment is insufficient to support normal levels of pay (Leslie, Kellams, and Gunne 1982, p. 76).

Enrollment-driven hiring of part-time faculty implies that they will be notified shortly before the semester or quarter begins, but the data are conflicting. A study of colleges and universities in Ohio shows that only a very small percentage of such part-time faculty were notified less than a week before classes began. Those faculty who were given more notice reported that they had time to prepare and that they were teaching courses they preferred (Yang and Zak 1981, pp. 11–12). In community colleges, however, 41 percent of part-time faculty indicated they were notified less than a week before classes began.

How do part-time faculty feel about enrollment-driven hiring?

Perhaps no gesture more clearly indicates the tenuous character of the relationship the university wishes to maintain with its part-time faculty than its form contract. In the nine years of my tenure as "Associate Faculty," I have accumulated more than 25 of these documents, for they are issued for each semester and each summer term, usually in the last two weeks or so before the first class sessions. In these contracts, I am "approved as an associate faculty member to teach" specific courses at a fixed "stipend.". . . After so many years and so many contracts, the opening paragraph seems to describe my experience less than my feeling of anxiety and the university's wish: "Associate faculty appointments are on a temporary basis in accord with University policy and are subject to cancellation if enrollment is inadequate. Also, if teaching schedules need to be reassigned because of low enrollment, priority will be given to resident (i.e., full-time) faculty." For many colleagues, both in my department and in others, distressing cancellations and changes of both course and schedule are not infrequent. In my own department, courses have been cancelled because of insufficient enrollment as late as a week after the semester began, which may account for the fact that our department's associate faculty contracts are never delivered until the second or third week of the term (Van Arsdale 1978, p. 196).

Regardless of the procedure used to recruit part-time faculty, the criteria most commonly used to judge candidates are practical experience, evidence of teaching skill, and availability to teach at certain hours. No responding institutions in one survey assessed either creative or research potential (Leslie, Kellams, and Gunne 1982, p. 75).

Assignment and Workload

Most part-time faculty teach one or two courses per semester. Eighty-five percent of the California community colleges surveyed limited part-timers to 60 percent loads, with the average being 30 percent (Sewell, Brydon, and Plosser 1976; Smith 1981; Tuckman 1978). Limits on available or permissible teaching loads cause some part-time faculty, particularly Tuckman's hopeful full-timers, to piece together a variety of part-time teaching positions at different institutions. The resulting schedule is rather hectic:

> *Three mornings a week I rise at 6 a.m., hit the road by 7 and drive an hour. I teach an 8 a.m. sophomore literature class, grade papers and prepare class plans until noon, teach a noon freshman composition class, dash back to my office (the pronoun is deceptive since the office actually also belongs to two other instructors, but I've never seen them—one's Tuesday/Thursday and the other is nights), pack up my books and papers and drive for another hour across town to another local university. I arrive there at 2 p.m., prepare, grade papers and hold office hours, then teach a 4:15 advanced composition class. On Tuesdays, Thursdays, and Saturdays I write my dissertation. On Sundays, I do marathon grading and take out my hostilities on my husband* (Chell 1982, p. 35).

A common phenomenon, particularly in the community colleges, is the employment of full-time faculty to teach an overload, usually in the evening program. In 1976, 53 percent of the full-time faculty in California community colleges were so employed; full-time faculty were given priority to teach on an overload basis in 82 percent of the colleges surveyed (Sewell, Brydon, and Plosser 1976, pp. 5, 11). A study at Los Rios Community College showed that over six years, the number of full-time instructors had increased 12 percent, while the number of part-time instructors had increased 480 percent. Much of this increase was in the evening division, where 46 percent of the daytime faculty taught an overload course because district policy gave them first choice of night courses. Almost half of the full-time instructors were working an overload at a time when significant numbers of part-timers were unemployed or underemployed (Ferris 1976).

Full-time faculty have resisted attempts to deprive them of their long-standing privilege to claim overload assignments. But in colleges where part-time faculty are members of the bargaining unit, it is becoming more difficult for full-time faculty to bump part-time faculty so that they might have an overload assignment. A few college policies and collective bargaining agreements already prohibit full-time faculty from being given overload assignments, and other institutions are placing tighter controls on the extent of such assignments (Lombardi 1975, p. 25).

Part-time faculty assignments involve primarily teaching. One study reported that 66 percent of responding institutions used part-time faculty for undergraduate instruction and 53 percent for evening and weekend instruction. Part-time faculty are also used extensively for laboratory instruction and noncredit or off-campus courses. Part-timers provide 28 percent of undergraduate instruction and 21 percent of graduate instruction (Leslie, Kellams, and Gunne 1982, p. 21). In Ohio, the findings were similar. Most part-time faculty taught basic lower division or general introductory courses. Fifteen percent taught upper division courses, 13 percent taught professional, specialized courses, and 5 percent taught graduate courses (Yang and Zak 1981, p. 11).

Full-time faculty have resisted attempts to deprive them of their . . . privilege to claim overload assignments.

Support Services

Part-time faculty very rarely enjoy a level of support for their work commensurate with that provided full-timers. Part-timers spend an average of $17\frac{1}{2}$ hours each week in activities related to their employment. About five hours are devoted to classroom teaching, a similar amount to preparation, usually at home. Research takes less than two hours, and advising or counseling students and all other departmental and institutional responsibilities occupy less

than two hours of the part-timer's time each week (Tuckman and Vogler 1978, p. 73).

Of the part-time faculty surveyed, 57 percent had no
office at all; 79 percent of them felt none was needed, however. Thirty-two percent of the respondents shared an
office with someone else, while the remaining 11 percent
had private offices. Overall, about 78 percent of the part-
timers in Tuckman's study believed that the facilities available to them were adequate (Tuckman and Vogler 1978, p.
74). But other sources indicate much more dissatisfaction
on this score. Some part-time faculty use office facilities
associated with their primary employment. If they hold
responsible positions in other occupations and their teaching at the local college or university is viewed as prestigious, the other employers may provide space, time,
and secretarial support (Leslie, Kellams, and Gunne 1982,
p. 81).

One method of providing space for part-time faculty has
been termed the "bullpen." The rationale is simple. If the
faculty member teaches one-fifth of a normal load, then he
or she needs only one-fifth of an office. This approach obviously impairs tutoring and advising students. In addition,
the absence of adequate office space for part-time faculty
blatantly informs students that they have second-rate status. Status can be a serious problem when the teacher
deals with nontraditional students who see office space as a
measure of success (Greenwood 1980, p. 56). Part-timers
frequently hold "office hours" in campus coffee shops,
student lounges, or even their homes. Some students are
discouraged by this arrangement. Moreover, the lack of
office space may impede interaction between part-time
faculty and other faculty and inhibit part-timers' identification with the institution.

Telephones, secretarial help, and graduate assistants are
seldom available to part-time faculty on the same basis that
they are for full-time faculty. Part-timers frequently use
their own phones, postage stamps, and typewriters. This
situation is partially because part-timers frequently teach
off campus, during evening hours, or on weekends, so that
they are simply not on campus when support services are
available (Leslie, Kellams, and Gunne 1982, pp. 80–81).

The lack of office space and support services is one of
the most persistent sources of frustration and anger found

among part-time faculty (Leslie, Kellams, and Gunne 1982). Wanting to do their job well, part-time faculty feel blocked by their lack of access to basic resources. Thus, institutions may save on direct costs of space but encounter indirect costs in the resulting frustrations and time wasted (Abel 1976; Leslie, Kellams, and Gunne 1982; Tuckman and Vogler 1978).

At our new campus . . . approximately 200 part-time faculty members from all departments . . . have "offices" in one large room divided into some 20 six by six–foot cubicles, each made smaller by the presence of two four-drawer filing cabinets, a flat-top table with a single drawer, and two chairs. University space is always costly and in short supply, but six to ten part-time faculty assigned to if not literally crowded into each six-foot-square cubicle would not represent a reasonable cost benefit to a university that truly valued its teaching staff.

Should concern with space seem unduly petty for professional people, consider the following: Only the single assigned file drawer can be considered the teacher's private office space. Only it is lockable. . . . Only one telephone is provided for the use of all part-time teachers assigned to this room. Until recently, no staff receptionist was provided to answer it regularly, so it was usually either in use or incessantly ringing. Only a single half-time secretary is available to part-time faculty. Departmental secretaries are unavailable. Obviously, most of my colleagues type their own copy . . . and generally do all of their own secretarial work. . . . Office supplies are simply not provided, although one may personally fetch rubber bands, paper clips, file folders, index cards, yellow pads, and note pads from one's department hoard, sometimes being called to give an accounting to the departmental secretary. Most bring their own. . . .

Part-time faculty experience these and other similar aspects of their working conditions as expressing the university's disdain and disregard for their professional roles and their personal dignity (Van Arsdale 1978, p. 197).

Community colleges provide far more opportunities for instructional development, support services, and orientation for part-time faculty than do four-year colleges and universities, in part, perhaps, because they employ greater numbers of part-timers (Greenwood 1980; Parsons 1980b). Development and orientation programs encourage part-timers to use available services. In contrast, Illinois State University spent well over $1 million from 1972 to 1978 to support more than 260 projects designed to improve instruction. More than 800 regular faculty (30 to 40 percent of the total) applied for support. The program was also open to temporary faculty, who amounted to about one-third of the total faculty and generated about one-fourth of all instructional credit hours. But during any given year, fewer than 6 percent of the part-timers requested support from the program; the average was close to 3 percent (Jabker and Halinski 1978).

Because the primary function of part-time faculty is teaching, nominal support for research is to be expected. A 1977 survey of part-timers teaching in the field of biomedical science showed that fewer than half were eligible to apply for research support or to be a principal investigator. In the three years before 1977, fewer than one in five such faculty applied for research support, and only one in 10 actually received support as a principal investigator (Atelsek and Gomberg 1980, pp. 7–8).

Communication with Peers and Participation in Governance
Contact with peers among full-time faculty is natural and free flowing. For part-time faculty, the contrast can be chilling.

> *Rushing in at about 7:30 one morning, I noticed a faculty member coming out of the office, about to shut the door, which wouldn't be reopened till the secretaries got in at 8:30. "Oh, don't shut that door. May I get in the office for a minute?" "Well, I suppose so," he said, looking me up and down and obviously wondering who I was and what I wanted. "I'll just grab my mail," I explained, doing just that and dashing right back out of the office, making no attempt to steal a typewriter. "Oh," he said, "do you teach here?" He had the grace to blush and try to cover the incident with a joke. "Well, I'm sorry but we do try to step on you part-timers as often as possible, you know." "Yes," I said, not taking a joke*

*very well at 7:30. "And you do it quite often and with
great effect"* (Chell 1982, p. 39).

Because of the lack of office space and opportunity to
meet informally with peers, part-timers may feel devoid of
status in the academic community.

*The most common problem for the adjunct is the relative
difficulty of communication. Unlike the regular faculty,
he does not have lunch, coffee breaks, and casual con-
versation with colleagues or administrators. Being set
apart from this community, he can expect to receive
requests for information several days after the deadline
for furnishing it* (Beman 1980, p. 83).

The writings of part-time faculty indicate that many perceive the institution as bent on communicating its authority
to temporary workers who feel terribly insecure to begin
with and need no reminders about who holds power. Little
casual sharing of information is possible about teaching
methods, materials, and student problems. Being denied
access to valuable information, being kept in a state of
uncertainty about future reappointment, and being seen as
in a different status by full-time faculty can create genuine
fear in the part-timer.

*For those of us who need these paychecks to buy our
groceries, the whole system is ruled by uncertainty and
fear. . . . What if I have some trouble with a student? If
there is any controversy, you won't be rehired. Old
hands tell you to fail a paper for its comma faults, not
for obvious plagiarism, because you don't want to risk a
student's challenge. All this makes for teaching on tiptoe*
(Chell 1982, p. 38).

Part-time faculty are essentially disenfranchised persons
in academic governance. Most find few avenues through
which to exercise formal or informal influence over departmental or institutional decisions. To the extent part-timers
have any influence, it is generally at the departmental
level. Forty-two percent of the sample in Leslie's study
reported that part-time faculty had either a full or propor-
tional vote in departmental decisions. At the college or
institutional level, about one-fourth of the surveyed institu-

tions reported that they extended voting privileges to part-time faculty. More often, part-timers participate in governance as observers or with speaking privileges only. The situation varies little by type of institution, though there is some tendency for greater involvement in community college and liberal arts colleges (Leslie, Kellams, and Gunne 1982, pp. 86–87). In 1976, about one-fourth of part-time faculty participated in governance on the same basis as full-time faculty, with semiretireds (31 percent) and home-workers (41 percent) indicating the greatest degree of participation (Tuckman 1978, p. 311).

A good many part-time faculty express a great deal of satisfaction with their disenfranchisement and lack of involvement in the governance of the institution. But some legitimately need to limit their involvement because they have primary full-time jobs elsewhere. Whatever their status, some part-time faculty perceive committee work and the informal political ramifications of collegiate decision making as distracting and ungratifying drudgery. They can legitimately avoid time-consuming involvement without pangs of conscience (Leslie, Kellams, and Gunne 1982, p. 86).

Compensation
Salary patterns

Salary patterns for part-time faculty take three major forms: an hourly rate, a semester rate, and a prorated share of the salary paid comparable full-time faculty.

The oldest and still most prevalent pattern is the hourly rate. Each hour spent in class is counted as an hour for determining pay. For lecture courses, one credit hour equals one contact hour. For laboratory and technical vocational courses, one credit hour may generate two, three, or more contact hours. In special courses that involve unusual preparation, as in some advanced science courses or English composition, a contact hour is usually counted as more than one hour in computing pay. Many variations exist in the basic hourly pattern (Lombardi 1976).

The semester rate provides a fixed sum per credit or contact hour per semester. Calendar days and clock hours actually worked do not affect the stipend, sometimes called an honorarium. Semester rates tend to be slightly higher than hourly rates for the same periods of time and are more likely to include fringe benefits.

The prorated schedule is computed as a fraction of the current salary for full-time faculty. The salary may be prorated across the range of the salary schedule for full-timers, matching column and step to the academic qualifications and experience of the part-time instructor, or it may be based on a particular column of the full-time salary schedule, usually at some point between the lowest and middle rate (Lombardi 1976). Overall, one-fifth of all colleges and universities pay part-time faculty on a prorated scale. At colleges and universities with collective bargaining contracts, about 30 percent provide prorated pay for part-time faculty (Leslie, Kellams, and Gunne 1982, p. 78).

Strict prorating of pay for part-time faculty is not equitable for full-time faculty, because full-timers' salaries reflect time spent on a wide array of duties other than teaching. At major universities, only one-half to two-thirds of a faculty member's budgeted time may be allocated to teaching, with substantial time devoted to scholarship or research. If one assumes strict prorating of an annual salary, a part-time faculty member would be paid a fixed percentage of that salary per course. If one assumes, however, that the full-time annual salary to be prorated must be reduced by the percentage of nonteaching assignments carried by full-time faculty, then the prorated wage for part-timers would be reduced proportionately (Leslie, Kellams, and Gunne 1982; McCabe and Brezner 1978; Magarrell 1978).

Part-time salary schedules are included in most policy manuals and some collective bargaining contracts. Salary schedules may differ for full-time instructors teaching overload classes, for day and evening part-time faculty, for credit and noncredit courses, or for occupational versus academic courses. In addition, pay may differ by discipline. Occasionally, class size can affect the rate of pay (Ferris 1976; Lombardi 1976). Rates for full-time faculty teaching an overload course are sometimes higher than rates for part-time faculty. Occasionally, day part-time faculty are paid at a higher rate than evening instructors. The part-time or overload rate is never higher than the full-time salary rate, however (Lombardi 1976, pp. 77–78). The logic for the lower rate for part-time faculty is that full-timers' assignments include duties beyond the classroom.

But some part-time faculty contribute fully to the life of the institution, notably the hopeful full-timers. Usually part-timers who perform nonteaching tasks receive no compensation for them. For these and other reasons, a three-hour class taught by a part-time faculty member who receives an hourly rate of pay usually costs from one-half to four-fifths the amount of a similar class taught by a full-time instructor on a yearly salary (Lombardi 1976; Tuckman and Tuckman 1981).

Colleges and universities normally use more than one pattern of compensation for part-timers, employing one mode of compensation for 60 to 90 percent of the part-time faculty and other methods for the remainder. For example, a college may pay 85 percent of its part-time faculty on a per-course basis and most of the rest on an hourly basis as temporary replacements. A few may be specialized long-term instructors who are paid by the year. The more complex the institution, the more likely it is to use multiple bases of compensation. Almost all institutions pay part-time faculty on some kind of scale, with rates varying according to rank or discipline. Local market factors sometimes require marked departure from such scales, however (Leslie, Kellams, and Gunne 1982, pp. 77-88).

Variations in compensation among part-timers

Variations in compensation for part-timers are shown in table 10. The rate per course taught is derived by dividing the average salary in spring 1976 by the number of courses taught. This rate varies little across most categories, except for the full-mooners, who were paid significantly less per course, and the homeworkers, who were paid significantly more. The full-mooners contributed most to household income, and the homeworkers contributed least, however.

In no category did the majority feel they were paid at least proportionately to full-timers. The highest percentage of those who felt they were paid at least proportionately was among the semiretireds and the part-unknowners. Only 14 percent of the hopeful full-timers felt that way. Hopeful full-timers are the most likely to be sensitive about inequitable salary, probably because they are most likely to do nonteaching work without compensation. Additionally, about half of the hopeful full-timers with a full-time workload at one or more institutions are not included un-

TABLE 10
SELECTED CHARACTERISTICS OF PART-TIME FACULTY: SALARY

	Semi-retired	Student	Hopeful Full-timer	Full-mooner	Home-worker	Part-mooner	Part-unknowner	All Part-timers
Workload								
Average contact hours	5.5	5.6	6.5	3.7	6.5	4.3	4.5	5.0
Average courses taught	1.6	1.6	1.9	1.2	1.6	1.5	1.3	1.5
Average total hours	15.1	15.4	18.0	9.5	17.5	11.6	13.8	13.5
Income/salary[a]								
Average spring salary	$ 1,714	$ 1,650	$ 2,030	$ 1,107	$ 2,351	$ 1,591	$ 1,657	$ 1,600
Rate per course taught	1,071	1,031	1,068	923	1,469	1,061	1,275	1,067
Total own earned income	11,703	10,463	8,660	22,802	5,346	17,268	15,957	14,826
Total household income	22,883	18,454	18,555	27,990	26,161	24,861	25,361	23,410
Level of satisfaction								
Percent who feel they are paid at least proportionately[b]	41.3	25.9	14.4	31.8	35.4	25.0	43.5	27.8

[a]For 1976–77.
[b]Those responding "don't know" are excluded from the computations.

Source: Tuckman 1978, pp. 309, 311.

der a retirement plan, and more than three-fourths are unable to obtain life insurance coverage, unemployment insurance, workman's compensation, or sick leave (Tuckman, Caldwell, and Vogler 1978, p. 191). Hopeful full-timers and homeworkers have the smallest average personal earnings, probably the result of the emphasis in these categories on college teaching as the primary job.

Salary rates per course vary little across categories, but salaries do vary markedly for part-time faculty across types of institution. Salaries for part-time faculty averaged $2,691 at universities, $1,950 at four-year schools, and $1,165 at two-year schools per semester (Tuckman and Caldwell 1979, p. 746). Salaries also vary because of institutional policies involving questions about what fringe benefits should be extended to part-time faculty, whether they should be allowed to teach more advanced courses, what increments should be granted in recognition of graduate degrees earned, publications, and other scholarly activity, and what types of contract should be extended (Tuckman and Caldwell 1979; Yang and Zak 1981).

Salaries of part-time faculty are influenced by the location of the employing college or university, because many part-timers have limited mobility and recruitment is usually local. In many areas, a large number of skilled professionals are available to teach an evening course part time, which inflates the supply of part-timers in medium and large cities and can even saturate the market in places like Washington, Boston, and San Francisco (Tuckman and Caldwell 1979, pp. 745–47).

Whether or not women are discriminated against in the amount of salary they are paid is another question. In a comparison of all categories of part-timers at two-year institutions, women were paid more than men only in the homeworker category. Generally, women part-timers made some $3,000 a year less than their male counterparts. The differential between men's and women's salaries was the greatest among hopeful full-timers (Tuckman and Tuckman 1980, pp. 71–73).

Variations in compensation between part-time and full-time faculty

Are part-time faculty paid an amount equivalent to full-time faculty for the work they perform? This question is difficult to answer because no simple measures exist to compare the credentials and workloads of part- and full-time faculty. Nevertheless, several researchers have attempted to answer it (Lombardi 1976; Lowe and Taylor 1979; Tuckman and Caldwell 1979; Tuckman, Caldwell, and Vogler 1978; Tuckman and Katz 1981).

Over 70 percent of part-time faculty hold unranked positions, compared with 12 percent of full-time faculty. When unranked faculty are compared, little evidence suggests a differential in salary. If the comparison is made on the assumption that part-time faculty should have a rank structure equivalent to that of full-time ranks, however, it appears that part-time faculty are paid 25 percent to 35 percent less than full-time faculty (Tuckman, Caldwell, and Vogler 1978, p. 187).

Differences in the salaries of part- and full-time faculty arise from differences in the factors that set the salaries. Salary differentials might be accounted for by differences in education, experience, quality of institution attended, and related personal and institutional characteristics. Such characteristics accounted for more than 65 percent of the variation in full-time salaries across universities but only 20 percent of the variation in part-time salaries. Part-time salaries appeared to be influenced more by institutional policies and market differences than by personal skills and qualifications (Tuckman and Caldwell 1979, pp. 750–53). In addition, part-timers received no statistically significant salary increment for length of service. As full-timers do receive such increments, part-time faculty who retain their positions are likely to fall behind their full-time counterparts over time even if they are hired at the equivalent salary rates (Tuckman and Caldwell 1979; Tuckman, Caldwell, and Vogler 1978).

Low and relatively decreasing salaries for part-time faculty make them an attractive labor resource for colleges facing hard times (Leslie, Kellams, and Gunne 1982; Tuckman and Tuckman 1981). The differential salary scales have an economic effect.

It appears that part-time faculty are paid 25 to 35 percent less than full-time faculty.

Just how much of a Best Buy this university has is shown in the aggregate cost of faculty instruction: 40 percent of all credit hours, taught by part-time faculty, cost only 1.2 million dollars, while 7.25 million is spent on the 60 percent of credit hours taught by full-time faculty (Van Arsdale 1978, p. 200).

A course taught by part-time faculty averaged $1,120, compared to $2,240 for full-time faculty. Cost per student credit hour was $10 for part-timers, compared to $40 for full-timers. This pattern held for each university studied (Lowe and Taylor 1979, pp. 13–20). This study did not take into account the different functions and responsibilities of part- and full-time faculty, however.

Separate labor markets exist for part- and full-time faculty, and the rewards for their productive efforts are not the same (Tuckman and Caldwell 1979). Neither the skills part-timers possess nor the skills they develop have a consistent, statistically significant effect on their salaries. Part-timers who hold a full-time job elsewhere are unlikely to be significantly influenced by the amount of their part-time salary. The same is true for those people who are only temporarily part time and for those who are semiretired. If the number of part-time faculty continues to grow and if institutions continue to pay them according to established practices, however, an increasing number of part-timers will be increasingly dissatisfied with their compensation (Tuckman and Caldwell 1979, pp. 756–59).

It is still unknown what effect legislation and court decisions outside academe on comparable worth will have on institutional policies and practices related to the compensation of part-time faculty. It is possible that comparable worth could have a considerable impact on the salaries of part-time faculty in the near future, making much of the current literature obsolete.

Fringe Benefits
Most part-time faculty who work less than half-time do not receive fringe benefits. Unless part-time faculty have access through second jobs to fringe benefits, the savings to the institutions today may be offset by higher costs to the part-time faculty and their families in the future (Tuckman and Vogler 1978, p. 73).

Group fringe benefits fall into two large categories: *retirement benefits,* including social security, retirement plans, and life insurance, and *health benefits,* including medical insurance, workman's compensation, and sick leave. While over 75 percent of full-time faculty receive retirement and health benefits, the benefits part-time faculty receive, either through academe or through their second employer, vary widely. Some part-time faculty are treated as consultants and are given no fringe benefits. In a limited number of cases, part-time benefits are established in proportion to workload. Part-time faculty working more than half time tend to receive more fringe benefits than part-timers working less than half time (Tuckman and Vogler 1979, p. 46). Table 11 shows the percentage of institutions in which part-time faculty are eligible for fringe benefits.

Fewer than half of part-time faculty Tuckman surveyed in 1976–77 were covered by social security in their academic position, and almost a third reported no social security coverage from any employment. Assuming that part-timers have adequate fringe benefits from a second position has its limitations. For example, social security coverage on a second job relates only to earnings on that job, not total earnings, and workman's compensation for a second job is not protection against injuries sustained on the first job (Tuckman and Vogler 1979, pp. 47–49).

TABLE 11
FRINGE BENEFITS FOR PART-TIME FACULTY

	Percentage of Institutions Reporting Fringe Benefits Available To:		
	Full-time Faculty	*Part-time Faculty More Than Half Time*	*Part-time Faculty Less Than Half Time*
Retirement plan	95.6	34.8	12.5
Medical insurance	96.3	31.9	6.3
Life insurance	84.1	23.2	2.8
Unemployment insurance	76.6	42.7	39.4
Workmen's compensation	86.2	53.2	52.4

Source: Tuckman and Vogler 1978, p. 77.

Unemployment insurance and social security are federal, statutory benefits. But workman's compensation and unemployment insurance are for the most part controlled by the states, which are generally free to establish their own rules and regulations for eligibility and disqualification (National Association 1983). Legislation prorating these benefits for part-time workers and changing requirements for workman's compensation and unemployment insurance would save institutions many dollars in actual costs, cut administrative bookkeeping and paperwork, and make hiring part-time professionals a more attractive alternative (Hine and Latack 1978, p. 101).

Job Security
Part-time faculty have little or no property rights to their jobs. Their hiring is often conditional. When a part-timer's course fails to meet minimum enrollment, the course is likely to be dropped and the part-timer dismissed. If a full-timer's load cannot be met without adding a course or a section, the part-timer may be "bumped"—that is, released to accommodate the change. At most institutions, part-timers are subjected to indiscriminate bumping at registration. Only 25 percent of the institutions in one study stated that they did not bump contracted part-timers in favor of full-timers. Thirty percent had no rule on this practice, another 25 percent permitted it, and about 9 percent attempted to find other duties for full-timers before bumping part-timers. The part-timer's seniority is no protection. Part-timers claimed that bumping was common and a source of extreme frustration (Leslie, Kellams, and Gunne 1982, pp. 88–89).

Probationary faculty in tenure-track positions are given appropriate notice regarding their contract status; the contracts do not simply run out. In contrast, faculty not eligible for tenure have no right to a presumption that their contracts will be renewed even if they perform well, because their appointment is based upon enrollment. It is common practice to give such faculty no notice and no reasons for dismissal (Thomson and Sandalow 1978).

Various alternative ways to provide additional security to part-time faculty have been suggested. They include giving part-timers all the benefits, opportunities, and responsibilities that they would receive as full-time employees: prorated fringe benefits, committee and advising assignments, tenure, and accrual toward sabbatical leave. Feminists see this kind of part-time appointment as benefiting working parents and enhancing the professionalism of the part-time faculty (Albert and Watson 1980; Gray 1977; Project on the Status 1976).

One alternative to the chancy career of a typical part-time faculty member is the practice of sharing a full-time position by two people who together perform that job (Project on the Status 1976, p. 3). Some institutions allow tenure for this type of part-time employment; others do not. In some cases, the people who share the position decide how to divide the teaching and other responsibilities; in other cases, departmental needs determine how the workload is divided. Institutions that have made shared appointments available to their faculty include Bucknell University, Hamline University, Hampshire College, and Wells College.

Another alternative is to allow mobility from full-time to part-time status and back again. Some institutions, such as Wesleyan University, help faculty members with young children or in the recuperative stages of an illness to continue their professional careers on flexible time. Institutions that allow flexibility in shared faculty appointments or time base generally provide access to tenure, sabbatical leave, and full voting privileges in the department.

In 1980, the College and University Personnel Association (CUPA) surveyed 795 institutions about their policies and practices regarding tenure and retrenchment. They found that tenure is rarely awarded to a person in a part-time, temporary role, but 14 percent of the institutions surveyed offered tenure to part-time continuing faculty. In those institutions, eligibility for tenure imposed the same requirements involved in tenure decisions for full-time faculty on part-time faculty (CUPA 1980).

Ineligibility for tenure is not limited to part-time faculty. Nontenure appointments, either part or full time, are commonly offered to accommodate scholars or artists in residence, replace faculty on leave, or meet temporary, often unexpected, demands for specialized courses over a short term. Some colleges have now extended the concept of nontenure appointments to full-time faculty expected to continue in their positions for fixed contractual periods

(Chait and Ford 1982, p. 68). A nontenure contract is common for research faculty who have a variety of titles and are supported either wholly or in part by extrainstitutional funds.

The CUPA survey found that only 54 percent of the public institutions and 38 percent of the private institutions had a policy on retrenchment. Among the 224 institutions that selected faculty for retrenchment, 61 percent of the public institutions and 50 percent of the private institutions had a procedure that involved designating specific academic units for reduction or elimination before designating the faculty to be reduced. Part-time faculty were selected before full-time faculty, and tenured faculty were selected last. Only 14 percent of the institutions reported that their policies on retrenchment required achievements in affirmative action to be maintained (CUPA 1980, pp. 141–42).

The CUPA survey showed that institutional policies and practices for retrenchment conform with academic tradition and such constraints as collective bargaining contracts and state funding requirements. For example, community colleges in California felt the effects of Proposition 13 immediately, because about one-third of their funding came from local property taxes. Administrators and trustees hastily canceled summer school, reduced the number of courses offered for the fall, increased the size of classes, and laid off 7,000 part-time faculty (just under one-fourth of the total). But the number of full-time faculty declined by only 2 percent. In fact, some of the part-time faculty who were laid off were actually full-time faculty teaching an overload (Abel 1979, p. 11).

That experience underscores what part-timers have long known: The primary feature of their status in higher education is their expendability.

PART-TIMERS IN TWO-YEAR COLLEGES:
Assessing and Improving Performance

Comparative Effectiveness

Nationally, 53 percent of the faculty at community colleges are part-timers (Eliason 1980, p. 2; Tuckman 1978, p. 313). The quality of their teaching performance is a major determinant of the institution's effectiveness. At the convention of the American Association of Community and Junior Colleges in 1979, the issue of standards for part-time teaching was debated with some heat. Proponents of high standards argued that part-time faculty should be trained not only in subject matter but also in pedagogy and professional ethics. Pragmatists maintained that two-year colleges have little choice but to take whoever walks in the door and agrees to work for "coolie wages" (Eliason 1980, p. 5). The convention did not agree upon standards against which the teaching effectiveness of part-timers could be measured. Among four-year colleges and universities, the question has never been formally raised in a national forum. Using what information is available, this chapter focuses on the efforts of two-year institutions to assess and improve the teaching performance of part-timers.

Judgments about the quality of instruction provided by part-time faculty, like all subjective evaluations, are influenced heavily by the perspective of the assessor. A mature adult student may place great value on the pragmatic outlook and real-world wisdom that many part-time faculty bring to the classroom—along with a tendency not to assign academic exercises that demand a lot of library research and written reports. Full-time faculty may see in this approach to teaching a damaging erosion of academic standards. A dean of instruction at a short-handed college with budget problems may choose to ignore questions about the quality of the part-time faculty's performance except in individual cases so conspicuously bad that students formally register complaints.

In any case, the quality of instruction by part-time faculty is relatively hard to predict. It may be superior, or it may be unacceptable (Leslie, Kellams, and Gunne 1982, p. 16). Very little objective information is available about the comparative effectiveness of part- and full-time teachers; what is available is about two-year colleges. And, taken together, the few studies that have been published are inconclusive. One in particular (Friedlander 1979, 1980) has generated controversy.

Friedlander's study examined the proposition that the instruction by part-time faculty is equal in quality to that of full-time faculty. He compared part- and full-time faculty on 11 criteria that he deemed likely to affect the quality of instruction. Friedlander analyzed data from national studies conducted by the Center for the Study of Community Colleges in 1975, 1977, and 1978. Some examples of the findings for various criteria follow.

- **Teaching experience:** Ninety percent of full-time faculty and 55 percent of part-time faculty had more than three years of teaching experience; 55 percent of the part-time faculty but only 13 percent of the full-time faculty had taught at the community college where currently employed for two years or less.
- **Selection of course materials:** Fifty-three percent of part-time faculty, compared with 11 percent of full-time faculty, stated that they had no control over the selection of textbooks used in their classes.
- **Use of instructional media:** Forty-five percent of full-time faculty, compared with 33 percent of part-time faculty, reported they used instructional media in their classes; 43 percent of part-time faculty, compared to 32 percent of full-time faculty, said they did not have access to production facilities or assistance.
- **Use of instructional support services:** Full-time faculty were more likely than part-time faculty to use clerical help (68 percent versus 51 percent), library and bibliographic assistance (43 percent versus 34 percent), and media production facilities or assistance (40 percent versus 31 percent). More part-time faculty than full-time faculty reported that these services were not available to them.
- **Availability to students:** Lack of office space and adequate opportunities and incentives to meet students out of class discouraged part-time faculty from trying to provide individualized support to students.
- **Involvement in professional activities:** Seventy-seven percent of full-time faculty and 67 percent of part-time faculty reported that they read scholarly journals, 82 percent of full-time faculty and 63 percent of part-time faculty belonged to a professional organization, 48 percent of full-time faculty and 38 percent of part-time

faculty had attended a professional meeting, and 11 percent of full-time faculty and 8 percent of part-time faculty had presented a professional paper (Friedlander 1980, pp. 29–34).

Friedlander concluded that differences between part- and full-time faculty were the result in part of differences in the education and experiential preparation of part-time faculty and in part of institutional policies and practices. For example, teaching experience and length of service at the college presumably are likely to enhance a faculty member's ability to conduct a course: It takes time for faculty to learn what instructional support services are available and to develop courses and effective instructional techniques. Because part-timers' employment is less continuous, it can be assumed that they do not have the same level of knowledge about the institution and the resources available to them that full-time faculty have. On the other hand, most institutions have not provided office space for part-time instructors to meet with students or adequate opportunities and incentives for part-timers to increase their understanding of the college. These factors inhibit part-timers' efforts to fulfill their extrainstructional responsibilities (Friedlander 1980, p. 33; Sewell, Brydon, and Plosser 1976).

If one accepts Friedlander's assumptions about what criteria affect teaching effectiveness, then one could conclude with him that the quality of instruction provided by a college is likely to be adversely affected as the proportion of part- to full-time faculty increases (Friedlander 1980, p. 35).

Others who have compared the teaching performance of part- and full-time faculty have refuted Friedlander's study. Hammons (1981) maintains it is unfortunate that the study that has received most attention (Friedlander's) used inputs as criteria (teaching experience, use of media, grading practices) rather than results achieved (performance in followup courses, attrition rates, changes in attitude). In the absence of more research, the issue will occasion no more than continued debate among researchers (Hammons 1981, p. 49).

Another study compared the teaching effectiveness and costs of full- and part-time faculty at pseudonymous Midwestern Community College. Three evaluation forms—for students, for faculty, and for administrators—were used. While some items differed from one form to another, the three groups registered no statistically significant differences in the evaluations of full- and part-time teachers. The researchers also discovered that part-time faculty cost considerably less than full-time faculty, no matter what measures of output were used. They concluded that at Midwestern Community College, part-timers are as effective as full-timers and at lower cost (Cruise, Furst, and Klimes 1980, pp. 54–56).

Another study examined the instructional effectiveness of the full- and part-time faculty at Elgin Community College in Illinois. The variables measured were students' ratings of teachers' effectiveness, class retention rates, and subsequent student achievement in advanced courses. Class retention was calculated by dividing total enrollment in the class after the first week by the number of students who received passing grades in the course. Students' achievement in subsequent courses was measured by comparing grades earned in initial courses with enrollment and grades earned in more advanced classes in the same discipline. No significant differences were found between full- and part-time faculty for these three dimensions of instructional effectiveness. With declining enrollments and dwindling resources, administrators will be more inclined to increase the use of part-time faculty because they can be expected to deliver quality instruction to their students (Willett 1980, pp. 23–29).

At Hagerstown Junior College in Maryland, staff who developed the evaluation system found no significant differences between the evaluative data based on frequencies and those based on percentages. Later, they tested the validity of their instrument by comparing their results with those obtained by using the IDEA system developed at Kansas State University. Again, IDEA found no significant differences between full- and part-time faculty (Behrendt and Parsons 1983, p. 39).

While the information available that compares the teaching effectiveness of part- and full-time faculty in community colleges is minimal and inconclusive, it appears that part-time faculty by themselves do not detract from the quality of instruction and that they can enrich it greatly.

The key lies in how they are selected, supported, and assigned (Leslie, Kellams, and Gunne 1982, p. 140).

Orientation
Most part-time faculty are employed for their professional competence, not for their pedagogical training. It falls to the employing institution to provide adequate orientation, in-service training, and opportunities for faculty development (Grymes 1977; McDougle 1980; Smith 1980). Part-time faculty who are not familiar with community colleges need to understand their missions, goals, programs, and procedures and be aware of students' particular educational needs.

Most colleges and universities (84 percent in the survey by Leslie, Kellams, and Gunne) provide no formal orientation for part-time faculty. Community colleges do somewhat better as a group: About 31 percent reported providing some form of serious orientation for part-timers. Orientation programs must take into account the inherent nature of part-time employment. Last-minute hiring based on enrollment can mean the institution will not know who its part-time faculty are until the semester has begun. Efforts to notify and schedule informal or formal sessions are frustrated by part-time faculty who have primary occupations elsewhere and normally cannot attend during regular working hours. Thus, for many institutions the provision of a well-organized orientation program for part-time faculty is loosely organized and practically uncontrollable (Leslie, Kellams, and Gunne 1982, pp. 81–83).

Despite these difficulties, effective orientation programs for part-time faculty do exist. They have certain common elements. Responsibility for these programs is delegated to an assistant dean, a director of an evening session, or some other administrator. Handbooks about the institution are distributed. Formal and informal training sessions describe the college and its teaching methods. Full-time faculty often serve as mentors or contacts for part-timers who may need a supportive relationship (Leslie, Kellams, and Gunne 1982; McDougle 1980; Parsons 1980b; Smith 1980).

A study of community colleges in nine states found that deans and directors, department chairs, and part-time faculty all affirmed a need for orientation and development in the areas of evaluation, educational philosophy, students,

Most colleges and universities . . . provide no formal orientation for part-time faculty.

---

and teaching. The perceptions of deans, directors, department chairs, and part-time faculty differed significantly, however. Deans and directors responded most affirmatively to the need for orientation and development, while part-time faculty showed least perception of such a need. For all three groups across all five categories of need, however, an overwhelming majority of the 227 respondents supported orientation (Black 1981, p. 281). These findings agree with those of Smith (1977) in his study of the 17 New Jersey community colleges.

Two orientation programs have been selected from the large body of literature for brief description here because of their comprehensiveness and practicality. At Hagerstown Junior College in Maryland, the orientation program is one of six components of a development program for part-time faculty. Orientation begins with an employment interview conducted by the division head, who gives the part-timer teaching materials, course syllabi, and sample examinations. Part-timers are introduced to full-time faculty teaching related courses and encouraged to contact them if any problems arise. They are provided a tour of the campus, the faculty handbook, and a workshop where other faculty in the department are introduced and their functions explained and questions about the handbook can be answered. Part-time faculty are given identification cards and parking stickers. Finally, division heads assemble part-time faculty to discuss topical matters (Parsons 1980b, p. 49).

The orientation program in the School of Technical Careers at Southern Illinois University seeks to help part-time faculty relate their courses to other courses in the curriculum (McDougle 1980). It is held before each semester begins, and all new part-timers are strongly encouraged to attend. Key university personnel attend, including the president, dean of faculty, directors of academic divisions, dean of student services, business manager, and director of learning resources. At the orientation meeting, each part-time faculty member receives a grade book, a library handbook, procedures relating to faculty duties, guidelines for preparing course syllabi, procedures for submitting grade reports, sample copies of student evaluation forms, and information about payroll and how to obtain faculty office space, mail boxes, and parking decals.

After administrative details, the educational philosophy of the School of Technical Careers is discussed, emphasizing quality instruction and college-level work. Although the courses are specialized and technical, part-time faculty are told that they are offered by a college for credit and that they must make appropriate academic demands of their students. Part-timers learn about attendance and grading policies. They are encouraged to revise course syllabi as they perceive ways to improve them, they are told that they must submit copies of exams to the division office for placement in a permanent file of course materials, and they are told how to identify and advise students unprepared for classes. Finally, they learn how part-time faculty are evaluated. The orientation program ends with a tour of the school's facilities (McDougle 1980).

Development

Faculty development involves activities designed to renew, upgrade, extend, or change the professional and pedagogical skills of faculty. Most models of faculty development assume that the quality of teaching can be improved when faculty share information about their teaching methods and when good teaching is valued and rewarded. Most faculty development models are concerned with full-time faculty (Cole 1978). In their survey, Leslie, Kellams, and Gunne inquired about support for research, teaching improvement, and professional development. Overall, about one-fourth of the institutions surveyed made some effort to assist part-timers. Under 10 percent provided any meaningful research support to part-time faculty beyond making laboratories and libraries available to them. One-third of the reporting institutions did reimburse some travel expense for attendance at professional meetings and one-fourth assisted with teaching improvement (Leslie, Kellams, and Gunne 1982, p. 84).

Sixty-eight percent of 114 responding deans of instruction at 207 community colleges said they provided some professional development for part-time faculty; 30 percent had none. The most common activities were designed to help part-timers learn about college requirements. Only in a few cases were part-time faculty given opportunities to improve teaching. While 68 percent of the respondents provided some form of orientation, only 17 percent allowed access to professional development libraries, only 12 percent videotaped teaching for evaluation, and only 12 percent provided instructional development funds for part-timers. Seventeen percent of the responding deans replied that some form of compensation was given to part-time faculty for participation in professional development activities (Moe 1977, pp. 36–37).

Forty-one percent of the respondents stated that they were having problems administering the development program. The principal obstacles were lack of staff, financial constraints, a lack of interest by part-time faculty, and difficulty in finding a suitable time to present programs. The survey revealed administrators' general attitude of frustration with professional development projects. In most instances, the community colleges tended to adapt development programs for part-time faculty that were designed for full-time faculty (Moe 1977, pp. 36–39).

Despite the difficulties, the literature about faculty development programs for part-timers describes a variety of exemplary community college programs. Some were started with federal funding; others had only institutional funds. A few examples are described in the following paragraphs.

The comprehensive faculty development model used at Hagerstown Junior College has six components. Each addresses a need identified by part-time faculty in a survey conducted to determine how the college could assist them to become more effective teachers. The need to maintain communication between part-time faculty and the college is emphasized. Each part-time faculty member receives the weekly bulletin, which contains announcements of general interest to the college community. Part-timers are encouraged to notify their students of the contents and to submit their own announcements. The weekly bulletin is intended to reinforce communication among all faculty and to underscore the importance of part-time faculty to the college.

The college's media center works closely with part-time faculty, providing equipment, funds to rent audio-visual material, and personnel. Hagerstown also conducts instructional clinics where faculty address problems they encounter in the teaching/learning process. Part-time faculty are notified about the instructional clinics and encouraged to participate. Occasionally they chair a session. Topics include performance objectives, effective lecture techniques, increasing students' motivation, and diagnosis of teaching/learning problems. Part-time faculty are given stipends for participating in the clinic (Parsons 1980b, pp. 48–51).

Coastline Community College in California serves 105 miles of the Pacific Coast and more than 500,000 people. It is responsible for all off-campus instruction previously operated by the district's evening division. All but a handful of Coastline's 800 faculty members are part-time, hired as needed on an hourly basis. The college has no facilities of its own; it uses high schools and other community buildings. Instructional services include everything from photocopying instructional materials to speedy delivery of audio-visual equipment to teaching sites. Instead of the traditional series of departmental faculty meetings, Coastline's faculty confer at social events built around various themes; faculty often bring their spouses (Decker 1980, pp. 63–65).

At Vista College in California, also without a campus, more than 350 part-time faculty teach over 85 percent of the college's classes each semester. The college offers general education and occupational courses to 14,000 adult part-time students. While each faculty member has a program planner or administrator to contact with questions, he or she is essentially alone with the students out in the community. The small ratio of administrative support personnel to teaching faculty means that Vista College's part-time faculty must be able to perform well the multiple roles of public relations, learning diagnostician, instructional planner, teacher, counselor, and registrar.

Vista College was awarded a grant by the Fund for the Improvement of Post-Secondary Education to define and pilot test five components of a faculty development program for part-time faculty: audio-visual orientation, training seminars and workshops for small and large groups of faculty, a monthly faculty journal, individualized procedures for evaluating instruction, and part-time faculty consultants who provided technical assistance. The greatest challenge of the project was to design and provide a mix of services that would fit into the hectic schedules of part-time faculty.

The federally funded project developed a new handbook on teaching and learning resources and services and an orientation film for part-time faculty who could not attend regular sessions. A monthly journal emphasizing teaching and learning was produced. Seminars and workshops were developed: a nine-hour workshop on the issues and problems of teaching adults, a three-hour open house to introduce new and continuing faculty to the professional library materials and Vista College resources staff, an all-day seminar for faculty, including presentations by the college president and dean of instruction, and informal biweekly support sessions (Elioff, Whitmore, and Bagwell 1981).

Burlington County Community College in New Jersey employs 170 part-time and 110 full-time faculty. It began in-service institutes for part-time faculty in 1971. Participants are paid if they complete the work assigned and attend the sessions. Completion of an institute is one prerequisite for advancement to the status of senior adjunct faculty and higher pay.

The in-service training institutes consist of modules organized like courses. Subjects include the community college student, the institution's philosophy, the role of the community college in higher education, institutional facilities and services, and evaluation of students or courses. Participants in the institutes are required to complete all modules and to submit all assignments to the Office of Educational Development. They also participate in a written evaluation of the formal training sessions and the learning materials (Pierce and Miller 1980, pp. 38–44).

Siena Heights College, a small private institution in Michigan, also was awarded a grant from the Fund for the Improvement of Post-Secondary Education to experiment with a model for development of part-time faculty. Siena Heights enrolls only 1,100 students; it has 40 full-time faculty, with another eight or nine FTE faculty composed of part-timers (Maher and Ebben 1978, p. 74). In contrast with Vista College, Siena Heights wanted a plan for long-term development of a pool of qualified people who could sustain a continuing association with the college. Administrators believed that a program responding to the personal and professional needs of part-time faculty would enable them to build more permanent links with the institution. The aim was to reduce the high turnover of part-time faculty.

Program components were organized after a session to assess needs was held in which part-time faculty participated. Participants preferred three all-day Saturday sessions over other options. The first Saturday session was an orientation program, the second focused on teaching and learning strategies, and the third was an exercise in teaching. Each participant's teaching performance was videotaped in front of colleagues, and the videotapes were then critiqued. Although participants reported a great deal of anxiety about the experience as they were preparing for it, most rated this session as the most valuable part of the workshops. Many had no formal training for their college teaching roles; they included accountants, school teachers, social workers, psychologists, and artists.

A stipend was provided to encourage participation. Association of economic rewards with the development program proved so strong that Siena Heights College offered so-called growth contracts for part-timers. Under such a contract, part-time faculty receive increased pay in return for continuing participation in college-sponsored instruction and professional development programs. This effort was in keeping with the college's desire to develop a pool of part-timers with strong instructional skills on which the college could rely over the long term (Maher and Ebben 1978, pp. 81–86).

The common features of successful development programs seem to be a commitment from the administration, a structure that provides incentives for part-time faculty, a program based on an analysis of needs to determine what part-time faculty feel is essential to them, and conveniently scheduled activities. None of the programs described were extremely costly. As part-time faculty are usually an economy in themselves, it would appear feasible for institutions to assist them in learning how to become good college teachers.

Evaluation

Comprehensive evaluation programs for part-time faculty are rare in all sectors of higher education (Leslie, Kellams, and Gunne 1982, p. 83; Sewell, Brydon, and Plosser 1976, pp. 11–12). Most colleges do not have performance-based criteria for renewal of part-time faculty appointments, which makes part-time faculty much more vulnerable to random, offhand evaluative comments by students or other faculty (Maher and Ebben 1978, p. 79).

Only part-time faculty who have a continuing relationship with the institution should be evaluated. The college can expect that the continuing part-timer will gain greater insight into the nature and mission of the institution and the character of its students over time, will stay abreast of the discipline and new developments in pedagogy, and will serve as an advisor to students outside class. Evaluations of part-time faculty should also include evidence of the quality of work being required of and accomplished by students. In evening courses, both the faculty member and the students often are unwinding after a long day's work elsewhere. The temptation is strong not to insist on heavy reading assignments, essay tests, and lengthy papers (Maher and Ebben 1978, pp. 78–80).

A comprehensive evaluation plan should be designed to identify and reinforce desired educational outcomes. Just as the faculty member has a primary responsibility to deliver quality teaching, however, the college has an obligation to provide supportive working conditions and to promote professional growth for all of its faculty. Therefore, the institution must also evaluate itself as a supportive environment for part-time faculty (Maher and Ebben 1978, pp. 79–81).

Hagerstown Junior College illustrates these concepts through two-way evaluation. The part-time faculty member's teaching is evaluated, and the part-time faculty member evaluates the services rendered by the college. The results of both evaluations are assessed and used to improve the other five components of Hagerstown's comprehensive program: recruitment, orientation, communication, instructional development, and support services.

The Hagerstown model, developed over eight years, makes evaluation an integral and expected part of instructional practice. Faculty do not perceive it as irrelevant or as a threat (Behrendt and Parsons 1983; Parsons 1980b). Evaluation is first discussed during orientation, when the dean of instruction and the division chair interview the part-time faculty. During this interview, the expectations of the college are discussed and strategies for realizing these expectations explored. Evaluation is discussed again at the beginning of each semester, during the orientation workshop. Part-time faculty are reminded that evaluations will be scheduled at a mutually convenient time. Those who have participated in the evaluation process previously are urged to share their reactions with those who have not (Behrendt and Parsons 1983, pp. 36–37).

Part-time faculty at Hagerstown are evaluated in their first course and in alternate courses thereafter. At the start of each semester, the dean of instruction and the division chairs develop the evaluation roster. The evaluation consists of a student questionnaire and a classroom observation by the supervisor of classroom practices. The results of the student evaluation are tabulated and frequencies and percentages computed for each question. Students' comments are typed on a summary sheet, and the division chair reviews both components. At the end of the semester, a copy is sent to the part-timer with a letter from the dean of instruction explaining the meaning of the evaluation. If he has any questions, the part-timer is encouraged to meet with the chair (Behrendt and Parsons 1983, pp. 38–40).

Continuing review of the results of these evaluations showed that these teachers were well prepared in their subject matter but not as well trained in instructional techniques. In 1978, Hagerstown Junior College began a teaching workshop for part-time faculty under a grant from the Maryland Division of Vocational Technical Evaluation. Each annual workshop focuses on a different teaching technique (Behrendt and Parsons 1983, p. 40; Parsons 1980b, p. 51).

Community colleges have been the leaders in the orientation, development, and evaluation of part-time faculty. What works in community colleges may not work equally well in four-year colleges and universities—and may not work at all unless extensively modified. But most efforts by community colleges to improve the teaching of part-timers have capitalized on universals in human nature—the desire to belong, to do better, to be rewarded for improvement. It would not be overwhelmingly difficult for four-year colleges and universities to emulate those efforts in ways tailored to accommodate their different academic environments and goals. First they must acquire the institutional motivation to do a better job.

IN CONCLUSION: Some General Comments and Broad Recommendations

The steady increase over recent decades in the numbers of part-time faculty employed in the various sectors of American higher education is a complex phenomenon, both as to causes and as to effects. And the efficacy of this increase is hard to assess: Whether part-time faculty enhance or inhibit educational quality is speculative at best and largely determined by factors specific to each institution. Community colleges make the most use of part-timers and have been more concerned about their effectiveness and their professional welfare than have four-year colleges and universities. This concern notwithstanding, part-time faculty generally are treated inequitably in higher education. They are not paid commensurately. They work under substandard conditions. Their professional aims often are frustrated. They sometimes are humiliated by full-time faculty and administrators who deny them collegial status and consideration.

Some community colleges are making improvements, at least some of which could be duplicated at four-year institutions at little or no cost. Emulation of the efforts surveyed in the previous chapter would be appropriate in virtually all institutions. But it is not likely to suffice as a long-term response to the need to better serve the interests of part-timers and the need to help them better serve their students and their institutions. What follows is a set of general recommendations for further action.

With respect to part-time faculty, the first dictate of common sense is that the attendant problems cannot be solved if there is no institutional will to solve them. And where that will emerges, the suggestions offered here will likely seem as inadequate as they are obvious. Even so, these recommendations have yet to be acted upon to any great degree.

Nearly one in every three faculty are employed part-time, or more than a quarter of a million people (NCES 1980). Thus, their influence upon the quality and relevance of academic programs is a matter of importance to all concerned with the operation and effectiveness of higher education. The challenge of the 1980s and beyond will be to ensure that institutional policies and practices enhance rather than diminish the morale and productivity of part-time faculty. To meet this challenge, research about part-timers must be accompanied by changes in current policies and practices for the employment of part-timers.

The Information Gap

Despite their increasing numbers, little is known about part-time faculty. The latest data from NCES were gathered in 1976 and published in 1982. The latest data from the EEOC were gathered in 1977. Two major research studies of national scope, conducted in 1976 and 1978, should be updated. While numerous studies have been oriented toward type of institution, geographical region, state, or particular institution or issue, data from numerous smaller studies are neither compatible nor comparable, because no standard definition of part-time faculty is used and data collection is not coordinated. Currently, the most extensive information about part-time faculty comes from community colleges. Recent literature about faculty in four-year colleges and universities by scholars in higher education is predominantly concerned with full-time, tenured, or tenure-track faculty. Part-timers have been largely ignored. In summary, the available information is out of date and of limited use to administrators except where institutions have done self-studies.

Part-time faculty generally are treated inequitably in higher education.

Expanded research and dissemination of information about part-time faculty at the institutional, state, regional, and national levels can lead to recognition of their importance and to revision of institutional policies and practices for their employment. This information should meet the needs of administrators who determine how many and on what terms part-time faculty will be employed.

At a minimum, information that is national in scope and collected routinely by federal agencies should be current and provide data about the various sectors of higher education. As administrators base their decisions on the experiences of similar institutions, the HEGIS survey should be expanded to provide more information about part-time faculty at specific institutions. These data could be aggregated in various combinations to meet the needs of researchers, policy makers, and working administrators. NCES, EEOC, and other agencies have a responsibility to collect, process, and publish information that is timely and to promote standards for defining and reporting about part-time faculty so that the resulting data are compatible and comparable.

Institutional researchers and scholars of higher education need to examine part-time faculty employment as an integral part of their studies of faculty careers and working conditions (Brown 1982; Emmet 1981; Stern et al. 1981). Institutional research is needed to find out what institutional policies and practices (formal and informal) are in effect, what kinds and amounts of work part-time faculty perform, what support services are provided and whether part-timers know about these services, and what part-time faculty think about their working conditions. Mechanisms should be developed for sharing institutional case studies. Networks among professional associations can facilitate the rapid dissemination of information among institutions.

Policies and Practices
The supply of well-qualified people, the variation among part-time faculty, and the widely different ways in which institutions use part-timers all indicate that employment practices should be flexible. Institutional policies and practices should take into account the differences among part-time faculty in their qualifications, the functions they perform, and their contributions to the school's educational objectives.

Treating part-time faculty employment as a casual departmental affair rather than a planned institutional effort is rapidly becoming less feasible. If educational quality is to be preserved, the academic and financial needs of the institution must be balanced with legitimate demands from part-time faculty for improved status, compensation, and services (Head 1979). Freewheeling departmental autonomy should be replaced by centralized responsibility and accountability for part-time faculty employment to ensure fair and humane treatment (Leslie, Kellams, and Gunne 1982).

Institutions can develop an equitable classification plan that differentiates among part-timers, based on their characteristics and the reasons for which they were employed, and then develop policies and practices that reflect those differences (Head 1979; Leslie 1984; Project on the Status 1976; Smith 1980; Smith 1979; Stern et al. 1981; Wallace

1982). The challenge is not to achieve parity with full-time faculty. Rather it is for institutions to have clearly articulated, well-understood, humane, and equitable policies and practices, based on comprehensive knowledge about the differences among part-timers. Institutional policies and practices should place less emphasis on the polarization of faculty—full-time, tenured faculty versus part-time, temporary faculty. Instead, faculty employment should be seen as a continuum embracing the entire instructional staff, from full-time tenured faculty, to fully qualified continuing part-time faculty interested in their teaching careers, to contingency faculty hired to meet demand created by enrollment on a one-time basis. Individuals and institutions will be better served when different policies and practices are developed for different classifications of part-timers.

An important reason for emphasizing the differences among part-timers and the roles they play within institutions is the inconsistency of rulings by courts and labor boards. The best protection for colleges and universities is to clearly specify the conditions of employment for part-timers. Institutions should carefully develop contracts for the appointment of part-time faculty that specify the institution's requirements and the part-timer's rights. While part-time faculty possess few property or equal protection rights, they deserve thoughtful, deliberate, fair consideration of their interests (Leslie and Head 1979, p. 67). Where colleges and universities have had legal problems, it has generally been the result of their failure to provide or follow written policies and practices that take into account the diversity among part-timers and that govern all aspects of part-time faculty employment.

Whether or not part-time faculty should be included in the faculty collective bargaining unit has been an issue since academic collective bargaining began. Even when part-time faculty are part of the unit and covered by the collective bargaining contract, the treatment of their interests is usually less than equal, and full-timers are the primary beneficiaries of collective bargaining. Contract negotiations should be conducted with an understanding of the situation on each campus. Whatever the composition of the bargaining unit, the results of negotiations should be protection of those critical areas of concern expressed by many part-time faculty and a concomitant recognition of their positive role in the academic life of the institution (Leslie and Ikenberry 1979, pp. 25–26).

Part-time faculty have a very different status from their full-time counterparts. This difference is obvious in the institutional policies and practices for full- and part-time faculty for hiring, support services, participation in governance, compensation and fringe benefits, and job security. A strong case has been made that institutions should examine the effects of their policies and practices regarding part-time faculty employment and improve them consistent with their financial resources and sound legal principles (Albert and Watson 1980; Emmet 1981; Ernst and Mc-Farlane 1978; Head 1979; Hoffman 1980; Leslie, Kellams, and Gunne 1982; Parsons 1980a; Smith 1979; Stern et al. 1981; Tuckman, Caldwell, and Vogler 1978). Improvements are needed in the following areas:

- **Appointment:** Development of a qualified pool of applicants for part-time faculty positions.
- **Contracts:** Development of a contract for part-timers that articulates the institution's requirements while specifying and guaranteeing the part-timer's rights.
- **Support services and communication networks:** Emphasis on integrating part- and full-time faculty and on giving part-time faculty a sense of dignity and belonging to the institution.
- **Governance:** Erring on the side of inclusion rather than exclusion in faculty governance and departmental deliberations, particularly with regard to curricula, courses, and teaching materials.
- **Compensation and fringe benefits:** Provision of an equitable compensation structure for part-time faculty, based upon their qualifications, assignments, and performance; and provision of cost-of-living increases. Provision of fringe benefits for continuing part-time faculty.
- **Job security:** Thoughtful and deliberate treatment of the interests of part-time faculty in decisions about renewal, retrenchment, and dismissal. Appropriate degrees of job security for different types of part-time faculty.

- **Orientation and development:** Special programs to help part-time faculty become and remain effective instructors; access to regular faculty development funds or programs.
- **Evaluation:** Development of an evaluation system aimed at improving part-timers' teaching effectiveness that sets clearly articulated standards of performance as one basis for reappointment.

When all is said and done, many part-timers may fairly be characterized as the reluctant victims of a system that exploits them. Some are dissatisfied and articulate about their working conditions. Yet they persist and abide in higher education. Part-timers *want* to teach, and no one has persuasively shown that they teach with less good effect than regular full-time faculty. Moreover, institutions gain important financial and curricular advantages by employing part-time faculty. Most colleges and universities *want* them to teach, within limits that vary from one institution to another as well as across types of institutions.

These limits are not likely to be narrowed any time soon. It seems more likely that the supply of adequately trained and skilled part-time teachers will be more in demand. Individuals with advanced degrees who have little opportunity for a traditional academic career may increasingly seek opportunities to teach part time if this employment provides sufficient rewards, incentives, and personal satisfaction. The growth of proprietary and industrial in-house college-level training, particularly in high-technology areas, has begun to put entrepreneurs in direct competition with colleges and universities for part-time teachers. Higher education may soon lose much of its competitive advantage in this market, unless the lot of the part-timer in colleges and universities is substantially and visibly improved. In the long run, the latter alternative is almost certain to be the least costly and most beneficial to higher education.

REFERENCES

The ERIC Clearinghouse on Higher Education abstracts and indexes the current literature on higher education for the National Institute of Education's monthly bibliographic journal *Resources in Education*. Most of these publications are available through the ERIC Document Reproduction Service (EDRS). For publications cited in this bibliography that are available from EDRS, ordering number and price are included. Readers who wish to order a publication should write to the ERIC Document Reproduction Service, P.O. Box 190, Arlington, Virginia 22210. When ordering, please specify the document number. Documents are available as noted in microfiche (MF) and paper copy (PC). Because prices are subject to change, it is advisable to check the latest issue of *Resources in Education* for current cost based on the number of pages in the publication.

Abel, Emily K. 1976. *Invisible and Indispensable: Part-time Teachers in California Community Colleges.* Santa Monica, Cal.: Santa Monica College. ED 132 984. 58 pp. MF–$1.17; PC–$7.24.

———. 1979. "The View from the Bottom: The Impact of Proposition 13 on Part-time Faculty." Paper presented at the annual conference of the Modern Language Association, 29 December, San Francisco. ED 181 950. 19 pp. MF–$1.17; PC–$3.74.

Albert, Louis S., and Watson, Rollen J. 1980. "Mainstreaming Part-time Faculty: Issue or Imperative?" In *Using Part-time Faculty Effectively,* edited by Michael H. Parsons. New Directions for Community Colleges No. 30. San Francisco: Jossey-Bass. ED 188 717. 115 pp. MF–$1.17; PC–$11.12.

Andes, John. 1981. "The Legal Position of Part-time Faculty." In *Part-time Faculty in Colleges and Universities.* Current Issues in Higher Education No. 4. Washington, D.C.: American Association for Higher Education. ED 213 326. 21 pp. MF–$1.17; PC not available EDRS.

Atelsek, Frank J., and Gomberg, Irene L. 1980. *Tenure Practices at Four-year Colleges and Universities.* Higher Education Panel Report No. 48. Washington, D.C.: American Council on Education. ED 190 015. 49 pp. MF–$1.17; PC–$5.49.

Baldridge, J. Victor; Kemerer, Frank R.; and Associates. 1981. *Assessing the Impact of Faculty Collective Bargaining.* AAHE-ERIC Higher Education Research Report No. 8. Washington, D.C.: American Association for Higher Education. ED 216 653. 66 pp. MF–$1.17; PC–$7.24.

Baratz, Morton S. January 1978. "Making Room for Junior Scholars." *Academe* 12.

Behrendt, Richard L., and Parsons, Michael H. 1983. "Evaluation of Part-time Faculty." In *Evaluating Faculty and Staff,* edited by A. Smith. New Directions for Community Colleges No. 4. San Francisco: Jossey-Bass. ED 225 633. 123 pp. MF–$1.17; PC–$11.12.

Beman, Richard R. 1980. "Observations of an Adjunct Faculty Member." In *Using Part-time Faculty Effectively*, edited by Michael H. Parsons. New Directions for Community Colleges No. 30. San Francisco: Jossey-Bass. ED 188 717. 115 pp. MF–$1.17; PC–$11.12.

Black, Lynda K. April-June 1981. "Part-time Community Colleges Faculty: Their Needs for Instruction-Related Assistance." *Community/Junior College Research Quarterly* 5: 275–85.

Blackburn, Robert T. 1978. "Part-time Faculty and the Production of Knowledge." In *Employing Part-time Faculty*, edited by David W. Leslie. New Directions for Institutional Research No. 18. San Francisco: Jossey-Bass.

Brown, Grace Carolyn. 1982. "Part-time Faculty Effectiveness: Fulfilling the Need." Paper presented at the National Policy Conference on Urban Community Colleges, March, Detroit. ED 216 741. 7 pp. MF–$1.17; PC–$3.74.

California Community and Junior College Association. 1978. *Community College Instructors' Out-of-Classes Professional Functions: Report of a Survey of Full-time and Part-time Faculty in California Community Colleges*. Sacramento: California Community and Junior College Association. ED 154 873. 61 pp. MF–$1.17; PC–$7.24.

California State University. 1983. *Agreement between the Board of Trustees of the California State University and the California Faculty Association. Unit 3: Faculty. August 16, 1983–June 30, 1986*. Long Beach, Cal.: California State University.

California State University and Colleges. 1977. *Report of the Task Force on Temporary Faculty*. Long Beach, Cal.: California State University and Colleges. ED 165 642. 55 pp. MF–$1.17; PC–$7.24.

Cartter, Alan M. 1976. *Ph.D.'s and the Academic Labor Market*. Report prepared for the Carnegie Commission on Higher Education. New York: McGraw-Hill.

Chait, Richard P., and Ford, Andrew T. 1982. *Beyond Traditional Tenure*. San Francisco: Jossey-Bass.

Chell, Cara. January 1982. "Memoirs and Confessions of a Part-time Lecturer." *College English* 44: 35–40.

Cole, Charles C., Jr. 1978. *To Improve Instruction*. AAHE-ERIC Higher Education Research Report No. 2. Washington, D.C.: American Association for Higher Education. ED 153 583. 89 pp. MF–$1.17; PC–$9.37.

College and University Personnel Association. Fall/Winter 1980. "Tenure and Retrenchment Practices in Higher Education—A Technical Report." *Journal of the College and University Personnel Association* 31: 1–204.

Craven, Eugene C. 1981. "Managing Faculty Resources." In *Challenges of Retrenchment,* edited by James R. Mingle and Associates. San Francisco: Jossey-Bass.

Cruise, Robert J.; Furst, Lyndon G.; and Klimes, Rudolf E. Summer 1980. "A Comparison of Full-time and Part-time Instructors at Midwestern Community Colleges." *Community College Review* 8: 52–56.

Decker, Edward H. 1980. "Utilizing Part-time Faculty for Community-Based Education." In *Using Part-time Faculty Effectively,* edited by Michael H. Parsons. New Directions for Community Colleges No. 30. San Francisco: Jossey-Bass. ED 188 717. 115 pp. MF–$1.17; PC–$11.12.

Dick, Robert C. 1981. "Part-timers and University Faculty Development." Paper presented at the annual meeting of the Speech Communication Association, November, Anaheim, California. ED 210 713. 19 pp. MF–$1.17; PC–$3.74.

Eliason, Carol N. 1980. "Part-time Faculty: A National Perspective." In *Using Part-time Faculty Effectively,* edited by Michael H. Parsons. New Directions for Community Colleges No. 30. San Francisco: Jossey-Bass. ED 188 717. 115 pp. MF–$1.17; PC–$11.12.

Elioff, Ione; Whitmore, Lynn A.; and Bagwell, Richard. 1981. *Faculty Development for Part-timers: First Annual Report, September 1, 1980–August 31, 1981.* Berkeley: Peralta Community College System, Vista College. ED 216 737. 27 pp. MF–$1.17; PC–$5.49.

Emmet, Thomas A. 1981. "Overview." In *Part-time Faculty in Colleges and Universities.* Current Issues in Higher Education No. 4. Washington, D.C.: American Association for Higher Education. ED 213 326. 21 pp. MF–$1.17; PC not available EDRS.

Ernst, Richard J., and McFarlane, Larry A. 1978. "Are We Shortchanging our Students by Using Part-time Faculty?" In *Employing Part-time Faculty,* edited by David W. Leslie. New Directions for Institutional Research No. 18. San Francisco: Jossey-Bass.

Evangelauf, Jean. 18 January 1984. "U.S. Forecasts a 15-Percent Decline in Numbers of College Teachers." *Chronicle of Higher Education* 27: 20.

Ferris, Peter. 1976. "The Part-time Instructor in the Los Rios District: An Analysis." Paper presented to the Los Rios Board of Trustees, 3 March. Sacramento: Los Rios Community College District. ED 121 364. 14 pp. MF–$1.17; PC–$3.74.

Fink, L. Dee. Winter 1976–77. "Developing Temporary Faculty: The Challenge Posed by Teaching Assistants." *Educational Horizons* 55: 56–63.

Friedlander, Jack. Winter 1979. "An ERIC Review: Instructional Practices of Part-time and Full-time Faculty." *Community College Review* 6: 65–72.

———. 1980. "Instructional Practices of Part-time Faculty." In *Using Part-time Faculty Effectively,* edited by Michael H. Parsons. New Directions for Community Colleges No. 30. San Francisco: Jossey-Bass. ED 188 717. 115 pp. MF–$1.17; PC–$11.12.

Fryer, Thomas W., Jr. Spring 1977. "Designing New Personnel Policies: The Permanent Part-time Faculty Member." *Journal of the College and University Personnel Association* 28: 14–21.

Fuchs, Rachel G., and Lovano-Kerr, Jessie. 1981. "Retention, Professional Development, and Quality of Life: A Comparative Study of Male/Female Nontenured Faculty." Paper presented at the annual meeting of the American Educational Research Association, April, Los Angeles. ED 202 416. 26 pp. MF–$1.17; PC–$5.49.

Fulkerson, William M., Jr. 1977. "Resolving Retrenchment Problems within Contractual Agreements." In *Handbook of Faculty Bargaining,* edited by George W. Angell, Edward P. Kelley, Jr., and Associates. San Francisco: Jossey-Bass.

Furniss, W. Todd. 1978. "The Status of 'AAUP Policy.'" *Educational Record* 59(1): 7–29.

———. 1981. *Reshaping Faculty Careers.* Washington, D.C.: American Council on Education.

Gappa, Judith M.; O'Barr, Jean F.; and St. John-Parsons, D. February 1980. "The Dual Career Couple and Academe: Can Both Prosper?" *AAHE Bulletin* 32: 1–9.

Geetter, Joan. 1981. "The University of Connecticut vs. the University of Connecticut Chapter of the AAUP: Brief on Determining Faculty Workload in the Collective Bargaining Context." *Journal of College and University Law* 8(2): 254–67.

Gerry, Frank C. March-April 1981. "Three Issues You'll Hear More About." *Association of Governing Board Reports* 23: 35–37.

Goodwin, Harold I. 1977. "Part-time Faculty." *Collective Bargaining Perspectives.* Morgantown, W.V.: West Virginia University. ED 145 753. 5 pp. MF–$1.17; PC–$3.74.

Gray, Mary W. August 1977. "Report of Committee W, 1976–77." *American Association of University Professors Bulletin* 63: 141–45.

Greenwood, Richard D. 1980. "Making 'What's-His-Face' Feel at Home: Integrating Part-time Faculty." In *Using Part-time Faculty Effectively,* edited by Michael H. Parsons. New Directions for Community Colleges No. 30. San Francisco: Jossey-Bass. ED 188 717. 115 pp. MF–$1.17; PC–$11.12.

Grymes, Robert J., Jr. 1976. *A Survey and Analysis of Part-time Instructors at J. Sargeant Reynolds Community College.* Richmond, Va.: J. Sargeant Reynolds Community College. ED 125 687. 54 pp. MF–$1.17; PC–$7.24.

————. 1977. *Staff Development for Adjunct Faculty.* Richmond, Va.: J. Sargeant Reynolds Community College. ED 148 409. 15 pp. MF–$1.17; PC–$3.74.

Guthrie-Morse, Barbara. Spring 1979. "The Utilization of Part-time Faculty." *Community College Frontiers* 7: 8-17.

Hammons, Jim. Winter 1981. "Adjunct Faculty: Another Look." *Community College Frontiers* 9: 46–53.

Harris, David A. 1980. "From the President's Perspective: Part-time Faculty in the 1980s." In *Using Part-time Faculty Effectively,* edited by Michael H. Parsons. New Directions for Community Colleges No. 30. San Francisco: Jossey-Bass. ED 188 717. 115 pp. MF–$1.17; PC–$11.12.

Head, Ronald B. 1979. *Legal Issues Relating to Part-time Faculty Employment.* Charlottesville, Va.: University of Virginia. ED 174 060. 71 pp. MF–$1.17; PC–$7.24.

Head, Ronald B., and Kelley, Edward P., Jr. 1978. "Part-time Faculty and the Law." In *Employing Part-time Faculty,* edited by David W. Leslie. New Directions for Institutional Research No. 18. San Francisco: Jossey-Bass.

Head, Ronald B., and Leslie, David W. July 1979. "Bargaining Unit Status of Part-time Faculty." *Journal of Law and Education* 8: 361–78.

Hillsborough Community College. 1980. *Part-time Faculty Handbook.* Tampa: Hillsborough Community College. ED 194 124. 74 pp. MF–$1.17; PC–$7.24.

Hine, Peggy A., and Latack, Janina C. Spring 1978. "The Paradox of the Part-time Professional." *Journal of the National Association for Women Deans, Administrators, and Counselors* 41: 98–102.

Hoffman, John R. Winter 1980. "The Use and Abuse of Part-time Instructors." *Community Services Catalyst* 10(1): 12–18.

Hoffman, Lenore, and DeSole, Gloria, eds. 1976. *Careers and Couples: An Academic Question.* New York: Modern Language Association of America. ED 157 415. 64 pp. MF–$1.17; PC not available EDRS.

Jabker, Eugene H., and Halinski, Ronald S. 1978. "The Invisible Faculty in Higher Education: Temporary Faculty." Paper pre-

sented at the annual meeting of the American Educational
Research Association, March, Toronto, Ontario, Canada. ED
152 133. 26 pp. MF–$1.17; PC–$5.49.

Johnstone, Ronald L. 1981. *The Scope of Faculty Collective
Bargaining: An Analysis of Faculty Union Agreements at
Four-year Institutions of Higher Education.* Westport, Conn.:
Greenwood Press.

Kellams, Samuel E., and Kyre, Kenneth K. 1978. "Part-time
Faculty in Four-year Colleges and Universities." In *Employing
Part-time Faculty,* edited by David W. Leslie. New Directions
for Institutional Research No. 18. San Francisco: Jossey-Bass.

Keller, George. 1983. *Academic Strategy: The Management
Revolution in American Higher Education.* Baltimore: Johns
Hopkins University Press.

Kerwin, Jeffrey. 1980. "The Part-time Teacher and Tenure in
California." *Golden Gate University Law Review* 10(2): 765–
803.

Koltai, Leslie. September 1977. "King Solomon and the Bowl of
Spaghetti." *Community and Junior College Journal* 48: 18–20.

Leslie, David W. November 1978a. "Current Perspectives on
Part-time Faculty." *AAHE Bulletin* 31: 3–6. ED 165 511. 6 pp.
MF–$1.17; PC–$3.74.

———. 1978b. "The Part-time Faculty Labor Force." In *Employing Part-time Faculty,* edited by David W. Leslie. New Directions for Institutional Research No. 18. San Francisco: Jossey-
Bass.

———. 1984. "Policies for Part-time Faculty: Developments in
Law and Collective Bargaining." Paper presented at the annual
conference of the American Association for Higher Education,
15 March, Chicago.

Leslie, David W., and Head, Ronald B. Winter 1979. "Part-time
Faculty Rights." *Educational Record* 60: 46–67.

Leslie, David W., and Ikenberry, D. Jane. Fall 1979. "Collective
Bargaining and Part-time Faculty: Contract Content." *Journal
of the College and University Personnel Association* 30: 18–26.

Leslie, David W.; Kellams, Samuel E.; and Gunne, G. Manny.
1982. *Part-time Faculty in American Higher Education.* New
York: Praeger Publishers.

Lewis, Lionel S. November 1980. "Getting Tenure: Change and
Continuity." *Academe* 66: 373–81.

Lombardi, John. 1975. "Part-time Faculty in Community Colleges." Topical Paper No. 54. Los Angeles: University of California at Los Angeles. ED 115 316. 62 pp. MF–$1.17; PC–
$7.24.

———. January 1976. "Salaries for Part-time Faculty: New
Trends." *Community College Review* 3: 77–88.

Lowe, Elizabeth B., and Taylor, Alton L. 1979. "Part-time University Faculty: An Analysis of Worth and Salary Cost." Paper presented at the annual forum of the Association for Institutional Research, May, San Diego. ED 174 109. 31 pp. MF–$1.17; PC–$5.49.

Lozier, G. Gregory. 1977. "Negotiating Retrenchment Provisions." In *Handbook of Faculty Bargaining*, edited by George W. Angell, Edward P. Kelley, Jr., and Associates. San Francisco: Jossey-Bass.

McCabe, Robert H., and Brezner, Jeffrey L. 1978. "Part-time Faculty in Institutional Economics." In *Employing Part-time Faculty*, edited by David W. Leslie. New Directions for Institutional Research No. 18. San Francisco: Jossey-Bass.

McDougle, Larry G. Summer 1980. "Orientation Programs for Part-time Faculty Members." *Community College Review* 8: 20–23.

McLeod, Dan. Winter 1980. "Watching our Discipline Die." *ADE Bulletin* (66): 34–35.

Magarrell, Jack. 16 January 1978. "Part-time Professors on the Increase." *Chronicle of Higher Education* 15: 1, 6.

Maher, Thomas H., and Ebben, James. 1978. "The Margin of Quality: Selection and Evaluation of Part-time Faculty." In *Employing Part-time Faculty*, edited by David W. Leslie. New Directions for Institutional Research No. 18. San Francisco: Jossey-Bass.

Maryland State Board for Higher Education. 1982. *Trends in the Characteristics of Faculty at Maryland Public Institutions of Higher Education*. Annapolis, Md.: Maryland State Board for Higher Education. ED 217 794. 44 pp. MF–$1.17; PC–$5.49.

Mayhew, Lewis B. 1979. *Surviving the Eighties*. San Francisco: Jossey-Bass.

Mingle, James R., and Associates, eds. 1981. *Challenges of Retrenchment*. San Francisco: Jossey-Bass.

Moe, Jackie. Autumn 1977. "A Staff Development Model for Part-time Instructors." *New Directions for Community Colleges* 5: 35–46.

Mortimer, Kenneth P. 1981. "Procedures and Criteria for Faculty Retrenchment." In *Challenges of Retrenchment*, edited by James R. Mingle and Associates. San Francisco: Jossey-Bass.

National Association of College and University Business Officers. 1983. *Federal Regulations and the Employment Practices of Colleges and Universities*. Rev. ed. Washington, D.C.: NACUBO.

National Center for Education Statistics. 1976. *Projections of Education Statistics to 1984–85*. Washington, D.C.: U.S. Department of Education.

————. 1980. *Digest of Education Statistics, 1980.* Washington, D.C.: U.S. Department of Education. ED 202 085. 269 pp. MF–$1.17; PC–$22.14.

————. 1982. *Projections of Education Statistics to 1990–91.* Washington, D.C.: U.S. Department of Education. ED 222 996. 129 pp. MF–$1.17; PC–$12.87.

National Center for the Study of Collective Bargaining in Higher Education. March-April 1977. "Part-time Faculty in Two-year Colleges." *NCSCBHE Newsletter* 5: 4–8. ED 144 650. 6 pp. MF–$1.17; PC–$3.74.

National Research Council. 1979. *Research Excellence through the Year 2000.* Washington, D.C.: National Academy of Sciences. ED 181 832. 245 pp. MF–$1.17; PC not available EDRS.

Nollen, Stanley D.; Eddy, Brenda B.; and Martin, Virginia H. 1977. *Permanent Part-time Employment: The Manager's Perspective.* Springfield, Va.: U.S. Department of Commerce. ED 146 374. 122 pp. MF–$1.17; PC–$11.12.

Padgett, Suzanne C., and Schultz, Raymond E. 1979. *Survival Skills for Part-time Faculty at Pima College's Community Campus.* Tucson: Pima Community College. ED 197 777. 34 pp. MF–$1.17; PC–$5.49.

Palmer, Arvin. 1979. *Associate Faculty Handbook 1979–1980.* Holbrook, Ariz.: Northland Pioneer College. ED 181 951. 41 pp. MF–$1.17; PC–$5.49.

Parsons, Michael H. 1980a. "Future Directions: Eight Steps to Parity for Part-time Faculty." In *Using Part-time Faculty Effectively,* edited by Michael H. Parsons. New Directions for Community Colleges No. 30. San Francisco: Jossey-Bass. ED 188 717. 115 pp. MF–$1.17; PC–$11.12.

————. 1980b. "Realizing Part-time Faculty Potential." In *Using Part-time Faculty Effectively,* edited by Michael H. Parsons. New Directions for Community Colleges No. 30. San Francisco: Jossey-Bass. ED 188 717. 115 pp. MF–$1.17; PC–$11.12.

Pascarella, Ernest T. Winter 1980. "Student-Faculty Informal Contact and College Outcomes." *Review of Educational Research* 50: 545–95.

Pierce, Harmon B., and Miller, Rosemary T. 1980. "Burlington County College Development Program for Adjunct Faculty." In *Using Part-time Faculty Effectively,* edited by Michael H. Parsons. New Directions for Community Colleges No. 30. San Francisco: Jossey-Bass. ED 188 717. 115 pp. MF–$1.17; PC–$11.12.

Pollock, Art, and Breuder, Robert L. Spring 1982. "The Eighties and Part-time Faculty." *Community College Review* 9: 58–62.

Project on the Status and Education of Women. 1976. *Part-time Faculty Employment*. Washington, D.C.: Association of American Colleges. ED 167 022. 6 pp. MF–$1.17; PC–$3.74.

Quanty, Michael. 1976. *Part-time Instructor Survey*. Overland Park, Mich.: Johnson County Community College. ED 127 000. 24 pp. MF–$1.17; PC–$3.74.

St. John, Edward P. 1979. *Academic Disciplines of Instruction/ Research Employees in Missouri State-Supported Higher Education Institutions 1978–79*. Research and Planning Series Report 79-7. Jefferson City, Mo.: Missouri State Department of Higher Education. ED 180 343. 47 pp. MF–$1.17; PC–$5.49.

Sewell, Donald H.; Brydon, Charles W.; and Plosser, William D. 1976. *Report on a Statewide Survey about Part-time Faculty in California Community Colleges*. Sacramento: California Community and Junior College Association.

Smith, Milton L. 1981. *Part-time Faculty in Private Junior Colleges*. San Marcos, Texas: Southwest Texas State University. ED 211 141. 14 pp. MF–$1.17; PC–$3.74.

Smith, Richard R. October-December 1977. "Developmental Needs of Community College Adjunct Faculty." *Community/ Junior College Research Quarterly* 2:31–36.

———. 1980. "Can Participatory Programs Realize Part-time Faculty Potential?" In *Using Part-time Faculty Effectively*, edited by Michael H. Parsons. New Directions for Community Colleges No. 30. San Francisco: Jossey-Bass. ED 188 717. 115 pp. MF–$1.17; PC–$11.12.

Smith, Robert M. 1979. "The University and Part-time Faculty: An Interdependent Relationship." Paper presented at the annual meeting of the Speech Communication Association, November, San Antonio. ED 178 993. 16 pp. MF–$1.17; PC–$3.74.

Spofford,Tim. November-December 1979. "The Field Hands of Academe." *Change* 11: 14–16.

Stern, Carol S., et al. February-March 1981. "The Status of Part-time Faculty." *Academe: Bulletin of the AAUP* 67: 29–39.

Strohm, Paul. 1981. "Faculty Responsibilities and Rights during Retrenchment." In *Challenges of Retrenchment*, edited by James R. Mingle and Associates. San Francisco: Jossey-Bass.

Thomson, Judith J., and Sandalow, Terrance. September 1978. "On Full-time Non-Tenure-Track Appointments." *AAUP Bulletin* 64: 267–73.

Tickton, Sidney G., et al. 1982. *1982 Idea Handbook*. Washington, D.C: Academy for Educational Development. ED 223 134. 189 pp. MF–$1.17; PC–$16.76.

Torgovnick, Marianna. Fall 1979. "Freshman English: Observations of a Former Adjunct Professor." *Improving College and University Teaching* 27: 147–50.

Tuckman, Barbara H., and Tuckman, Howard P. March 1980. "Part-timers, Sex Discrimination, and Career Choice at Two-year Institutions: Further Findings from the AAUP Survey." *Academe: Bulletin of the AAUP* 66: 71–76.

Tuckman, Howard P. December 1978. "Who Is Part-time in Academe?" *AAUP Bulletin* 64: 305–15.

———. January-February 1981. "Part-time Faculty: Some Suggestions of Policy." *Change* 13: 8–10.

Tuckman, Howard P., and Caldwell, Jaime. November-December 1979. "The Reward Structure for Part-timers in Academe." *Journal of Higher Education* 50: 745–60.

Tuckman, Howard P.; Caldwell, Jaime; and Vogler, William D. November 1978. "Part-timers and the Academic Labor Market of the Eighties." *The American Sociologist* 13: 184–95.

Tuckman, Howard P., and Katz, David A. Summer 1981. "Estimation of Relative Elasticities of Substitution and Relative Compensation for Part-time Faculty." *Economics of Education Review* 1: 359–66.

Tuckman, Howard P., and Tuckman, Barbara H. 1981. "Who Are the Part-timers and What Are Colleges Doing for Them?" In *Part-time Faculty in Colleges and Universities*. Current Issues in Higher Education No. 4. Washington, D.C.: American Association for Higher Education. ED 213 326. 21 pp. MF–$1.17; PC not available EDRS.

Tuckman, Howard P., and Vogler, William D. May 1978. "The 'Part' in Part-time Wages." *AAUP Bulletin* 64: 70–77.

———. November 1979. "The Fringes of a Fringe Group: Part-timers in Academe." *Monthly Labor Review* 102: 46–49.

Van Arsdale, George. November 1978. "De-professionalizing a Part-time Teaching Faculty: How Many, Feeling Small, Seeming Few, Getting Less, Dream of More." *The American Sociologist* 13: 195–201.

Wallace, M. Elizabeth. Winter 1982. "New Policies for Part-time Faculty." *ADE Bulletin* 73: 47–52.

Whelan, Wayne L. May 1980. "The Legal Status of Part-time Faculty." *Lifelong Learning: The Adult Years* 3: 18–21.

Willett, Lynn H. October-December 1980. "Comparison of Instructional Effectiveness of Full- and Part-time Faculty." *Community/Junior College Research Quarterly* 5: 23–30.

Yang, Shu-O Wu, and Zak, Michele Wender. 1981. *Part-time Faculty Employment in Ohio: A Statewide Study*. Ohio: Kent State University. ED 205 140. 105 pp. MF–$1.17; PC–$11.12.

ASHE-ERIC HIGHER EDUCATION RESEARCH REPORTS

Starting in 1983, the Association for the Study of Higher Education assumed cosponsorship of the Higher Education Research Reports with the ERIC Clearinghouse on Higher Education. For the previous 11 years, ERIC and the American Association for Higher Education prepared and published the reports.

Each report is the definitive analysis of a tough higher education problem, based on a thorough research of pertinent literature and institutional experiences. Report topics, identified by a national survey, are written by noted practitioners and scholars with prepublication manuscript reviews by experts.

Ten monographs in the ASHE-ERIC Higher Education Research Report series are published each year, available individually or by subscription. Subscription to 10 issues is $55 regular; $40 for members of AERA, AAHE, and AIR; $35 for members of ASHE. (Add $7.50 outside U.S.)

Prices for single copies, including 4th class postage and handling, are $7.50 regular and $6.00 for members of AERA, AAHE, AIR, and ASHE. If faster 1st class postage is desired for U.S. and Canadian orders, for each publication ordered add $.75; for overseas, add $4.50. For VISA and MasterCard payments, give card number, expiration date, and signature. Orders under $25 must be prepaid. Bulk discounts are available on orders of 10 or more of a single title. Order from the Publications Department, Association for the Study of Higher Education, One Dupont Circle, Suite 630, Washington, D.C. 20036, (202) 296-2597. Write for a complete list of Higher Education Research Reports and other ASHE and ERIC publications.

1981 Higher Education Research Reports

1. Minority Access to Higher Education
   Jean L. Preer

2. Institutional Advancement Strategies in Hard Times
   Michael D. Richards and Gerald Sherratt

3. Functional Literacy in the College Setting
   Richard C. Richardson, Jr., Kathryn J. Martens, and Elizabeth C. Fisk

4. Indices of Quality in the Undergraduate Experience
   George D. Kuh

5. Marketing in Higher Education
   Stanley M. Grabowski

6. Computer Literacy in Higher Education
   Francis E. Masat

7. Financial Analysis for Academic Units
   Donald L. Walters

8. Assessing the Impact of Faculty Collective Bargaining
   J. Victor Baldridge, Frank R. Kemerer, and Associates

9. Strategic Planning, Management, and Decision Making
   Robert G. Cope

10. Organizational Communication in Higher Education
    Robert D. Gratz and Philip J. Salem

1982 Higher Education Research Reports

1. Rating College Teaching: Criterion Studies of Student
   Evaluation-of-Instruction Instruments
   Sidney E. Benton

2. Faculty Evaluation: The Use of Explicit Criteria for
   Promotion, Retention, and Tenure
   Neal Whitman and Elaine Weiss

3. The Enrollment Crisis: Factors, Actors, and Impacts
   *J. Victor Baldridge, Frank R. Kemerer, and Kenneth C.
   Green*

4. Improving Instruction: Issues and Alternatives for Higher
   Education
   Charles C. Cole, Jr.

5. Planning for Program Discontinuance: From Default to
   Design
   Gerlinda S. Melchiori

6. State Planning, Budgeting, and Accountability: Approaches
   for Higher Education
   Carol E. Floyd

7. The Process of Change in Higher Education Institutions
   Robert C. Nordvall

8. Information Systems and Technological Decisions: A Guide
   for Non-Technical Administrators
   Robert L. Bailey

9. Government Support for Minority Participation in Higher
   Education
   Kenneth C. Green

10. The Department Chair: Professional Development and Role
    Conflict
    David B. Booth

1983 Higher Education Research Reports

1. The Path to Excellence: Quality Assurance in Higher
   Education
   *Laurence R. Marcus, Anita O. Leone, and Edward D.
   Goldberg*

1984 Higher Education Research Reports